INDOCTRINATION

INDOCTRINATION

How 'Useful Idiots' Are Using Our Schools
to Subvert American Exceptionalism

By Kyle Olson

with Ben Velderman

Edited by Steve Gunn

A publication of Education Action Group

authorHOUSE®

AuthorHouse™
1663 Liberty Drive
Bloomington, IN 47403
www.authorhouse.com
Phone: 1-800-839-8640

First published by AuthorHouse   10/20/2011

ISBN: 978-1-4670-6057-8 (sc)
ISBN: 978-1-4670-6041-7 (hc)
ISBN: 978-1-4670-6058-5 (ebk)

Library of Congress Control Number: 2011918086

Printed in the United States of America

For Jack and Gavin

"America will never be destroyed from the outside. If we falter and lose our freedoms, it will be because we destroyed ourselves."

—*Abraham Lincoln*

Table of Contents

Foreword

It has become a truism for conservatives that the media and the entertainment industry are biased in favor of the left. We pick and choose the films we watch—or let our kids watch—and tune to *Fox News* to get at what is really going on.

Now comes Kyle Olson's new book *Indoctrination: How 'Useful Idiots' Are Using Our Schools to Subvert American Exceptionalism*, which exposes the third leg of the stool that keeps the left propped up in our politics: The systematic indoctrination of our children in the public and private schools of America.

Olson, a long time education reformer, presents chilling evidence of the left's attempt to ban Christianity and Judaism from the consciousness of our kids. He takes us through the chronically inaccurate rewrite of American history taught in our schools. We are the aggressor. America is not an exceptional nation, unless it be exceptionally guilty of crimes against humanity! In the world of our schools, American democracy is a fraud and our free enterprise system is a monopolistic conspiracy to hold down the poor.

Karl Marx could not have designed a curriculum any better!

Olson traces the migration of the extreme left from economic Marxism to "cultural Marxism," replacing the theory of class warfare with a culture war which pits revisionism against our best values and traditions. Freed from the moorings of our shared history and outlook as a nation, this cultural Marxism replaces the values of the melting pot with those of a stubbornly maintained cultural and linguistic diversity. It mocks the motto *E Pluribus Unum* (out of many, one) and emphasizes division, conflict, and competing interests.

We have become accustomed to hearing American history and politics misinterpreted by leftist university professors. In 2004, the president of Williams College was asked how his faculty voted in the recent election. *"One hundred forty-one to nothing for John Kerry"* was his proud answer. Campuses that bend and strain to maintain economic, gender, geographic, racial, ethnic and even sexual orientation diversity do nothing to provide balance in their teaching of history and politics.

But in Olson's book, we see the insidious indoctrination at the elementary and secondary school levels. At least university students can think for themselves and are soon to enter the real world where they can figure things out. But Olson explains how 7- and 8-year-olds are taught to embrace an atheistic, leftist philosophy virtually from the moment they enter school.

Worse, he emphasizes how we are paying for this indoctrination with our tax dollars and how we are being denied the option of finding a school that suits our values by the public school monopoly.

For defenders of freedom, Kyle Olson's book is a vital necessity to read and absorb. It sets a challenge before us all: To change public education so that it is truly American in its values.

—*Dick Morris*

Introduction

Give me four years to teach the children and
the seed I have sown will never be uprooted.
—Vladimir Lenin

If you don't think the United States of America is the greatest country in the history of the world, stop reading here. I don't want to be held liable for your head exploding.

Unfortunately, the concept of American Exceptionalism is no longer being taught in many of our schools. Instead, the mainstays of the progressive movement—union leaders, globalists, environmentalists and multiculturalists—are bringing their agenda into our classrooms in an attempt to plant the seeds of socialism in the minds of our young people.

Socialism is a mild form of Communism, which is rooted in the belief that individuals don't have a right to property or fundamental life choices. It runs completely counter to the fundamental ideals of American culture and society.

As you'll see in the following pages, the progressives are very subtle in their efforts to bring socialism into the classroom. A story of union organizing will be couched in a science lesson. Videos that promote "green living" actually attack free markets, not "global warming" or animal population decline.

What they have been teaching our children is already having an impact on our culture.

The real motivation: A shift in culture

During the "Red Scare," when Americans actually feared socialists and communists instead of ignoring them as we largely do today, radicals understood it was unlikely they could win elective office, at least to the degree necessary to control any legislative agendas. Besides, they reasoned, it would be too easy for their enemies to reverse those gains. There had to be a more subtle and equally powerful way of transforming America.

They decided to change American culture.

As Dr. Ted Baehr and Pat Boone explained in their book, "The Culture-wise Family: Upholding Christian Values in a Mass Media World":

> "What happened, in short, is that America's traditional culture, which had grown up over generations from our Western, Judeo-Christian roots, was swept aside by an ideology. We know that ideology best as 'political correctness' or 'multi-culturalism.' It really is cultural Marxism, Marxism translated from economic into cultural terms in an effort that goes back not to the 1960s, but to World War I. Incredible as it may seem, just as the old economic Marxism of the Soviet Union has faded away, a new cultural Marxism has become the ruling ideology of America's elites. The No. 1 goal of that cultural Marxism, since its creation, has been the destruction of Western culture and the Christian religion."[1]

What are the three main branches of culture that have the most dramatic impact on the way Americans think? Hollywood, the news media and education.

Public schools continue to be a battleground in the culture war, as the education establishment—composed primarily of leftists bent on political correctness (cultural Marxism)—gains more ground.

This strain of thought treats Christianity and its holidays, for example, as a pariah, while embracing Muslim holidays.

In the spring of 2011, the Hillsboro, Oregon school board held a vote on what to call the school vacation that occurs around Christmas and New Year's Day. It had traditionally been called "Christmas Break." But new calendars, produced by school staff, changed it to "Winter Break." In response, the school board voted 4-3 to change the name back to "Christmas Break." From OregonLive.com:

> "[School board member] Janeen Sollman said winter break 'respects everyone in the community. This isn't about religion, it boils down to respect.'
>
> "Later, Hillsboro Education Association president Kathy Newman sided with Sollman and reminded the school board that equity is among its goals and 'the district calendar should reflect that.'"[2]

Farther up the Pacific coast, a high school sophomore in Seattle explained to a local radio station that the term "Easter eggs" could no longer be used because the administration preferred "spring spheres."[3]

Spring spheres. Really? Is America being Punk'd?

Unbelievably, the trend caught on elsewhere in Seattle. The parks department's website had several listings for "Spring Egg Hunts" all over the city.[4] The word "Easter" had been wiped off the city's website completely.

But never fear: One religion, Islam, is being protected and gaining ground in American public schools. The *Boston Globe* reports:

> "But beginning next year, Cambridge public schools will attempt to make it easier for Muslim students to honor their highest holy days.
>
> "In a move that school officials believe is the first of its kind in the state, Cambridge will close schools for one Muslim holiday each year beginning in the 2011-2012 school year.

"The school will either close for Eid al-Fitr or Eid al-Adha, also known as the Festival of Sacrifice, depending on which holiday falls within the school year. If both fall within the school calendar, the district will close for only one of the days."[5]

And if you're wondering, the Cambridge school calendar denotes the existence of a "Winter Break." This is little more than cultural Marxism in daily practice.

This isn't just about holidays. The political correctness that has taken root in our public schools has also provided a platform for a radical anti-American ideology.

Far left teachers have young minds captured for 6 ½ hours a day and work subtly to fill them with Marxist and radical ideas. So how does one go about it? Not by flying the Soviet flag, nor by replacing Washington's picture with one of Karl. Those actions would be too overt.

At the recent socialist Left Forum, a New York City teacher explained how she incorporates socialism into her classes:

"Part of it is just actually allowing for room for critical thought in the classroom and allowing for students to think for themselves to talk about issues wherever it's possible to bring in history and you know . . . radicals from the past . . . fight for that kind of thing. And I think there is space to do that. There is [*sic*] limitations that we have to do to try to provide that room in our classrooms. I think that radicals and socialists have a particular role to play in fighting for that type of education and bringing it whenever possible . . ."[6]

According to historian William S. Lind, the Italian Marxist Antonio Gramsci called for "Marxists to undertake a 'long march through the institutions.'" This scheme seems to be working beautifully in American public schools.

Lind writes:

> "The student rebellion of the 1960s, driven largely by opposition to the draft for the Vietnam War, gave [Herbert] Marcuse a historic opportunity. As perhaps its most famous 'guru,' he injected the Frankfurt School's cultural Marxism into the baby boom generation. Of course, they did not understand what it really was. As was true from the Institute [of Social Research's] beginning, Marcuse and the few other people 'in the know' did not advertise that political correctness and multi-culturalism were a form of Marxism. But the effect was devastating: a whole generation of Americans, especially the university-educated elite, absorbed cultural Marxism as their own, accepting a poisonous ideology that sought to destroy America's traditional culture and Christian faith. That generation, which runs every elite institution in America, now wages a ceaseless war on all traditional beliefs and institutions. They have largely won that war. Most of America's traditional culture lies in ruins."[7]

A 2010 survey by the Bill of Rights Institute revealed that nearly half of U.S. adults thought a popular Marx saying—"from each according to his ability, to each according to his needs"—originated from one of our nation's founding documents.[8]

Karl Marx being confused with America's Founding Fathers? Let that marinate for a minute.

Their efforts to move America's culture leftward are succeeding. That doesn't bode well for our historically successful tradition of liberty and self-governance.

This is child abuse

If American public schools were at the top of the class globally, that might provide an excuse for lesson plans that divert attention away from the basics. But what we see throughout the nation is example after example of American schools failing our children. Our government schools squander billions and leave many children unprepared for life.

It's immoral. It should be deemed child abuse.

If we were a third world country that lacked money and basic resources, we might have an excuse for such a dismal public education system. But we are the greatest country on Earth. We spend hundreds of billions on education every single year, yet we are turning out graduates who cannot read.

Many American high school graduates cannot read this sentence.

This is America. There is no way this can be happening, right? Think again.

A few years ago, a front page story in the *Detroit Free Press* told the tragic story of Amiya Olden, a graduate of Detroit Public Schools. The problem? She couldn't read the words on the piece of paper she was handed on graduation day.[9]

What a travesty and a crime against our children. Our education system is so broken that year after year, a student like Amiya is patted on the back, probably told she's doing a great job and passed along to the next grade. It happens over and over and after twelve years, she's dumped off the assembly line, unable to accomplish the most basic of tasks. At the time it was published, the story was four years old. This must have been some sort of an aberration—someone who just slipped through the cracks, right? Unfortunately, no.

In the making of "Kids Aren't Cars," a documentary film series on the state of American public education (KidsArentCars.com), my team from Education Action Group revealed that thousands of illiterate Detroit graduates exist. The executive director of ProLiteracy Detroit, the clinic that helped Amiya, estimated her organization has helped 11,000 graduates learn how to read.[10]

To put this another way: Detroit Public Schools spends nearly one billion dollars a year and yet graduates thousands of students a year who are unprepared for life. In America, this is totally unacceptable.

This is a multi-pronged problem. There is a perception—largely promoted by those in the education establishment who are beginning to feel the heat—that a lack of parenting is to blame. That certainly must contribute to it. But I've yet to see a study indicating the "bad parenting" problem is worse now than 10 or 20 years ago. The bigger problem is the bureaucratic public education system that has become corrupted and unmanageable.

Education reformer Michelle Rhee, the former chancellor of Washington, D.C. public schools, has said it perfectly: Schools should operate from the position that parents will do nothing to help with their child's education.

Blaming parents is no virtue, and accountability is no vice.

The blame lies with administrators who are unwilling to remove ineffective and burned-out teachers. The blame lies with teachers unions that are more concerned with increasing pay and benefit levels for their members than they are about teacher quality. And blame lies with school boards that do not set high standards, or demand that all employees teach the approved curriculum.

So while student achievement is lagging and countries like Iceland and Hungary are kicking our butts, our children are being fed socialist propaganda. The intent of this book is to expose the problems and offer potential solutions.

HOW TEACHERS SPREAD
CULTURAL MARXISM

Partisan teaching . . . invites diversity of opinion but does not lose sight of the aim of the curriculum; to alert students to global injustice, to seek explanations, and to encourage activism.

*—Milwaukee teachers union President Bob Peterson
and Oregon teacher Bill Bigelow*

CHAPTER 1

Legislating the Curriculum

Politicians need lots of money to get elected and re-elected. That means they need wealthy special interest groups supporting them.

The politicians who accept the money find different ways to repay their sponsors. Often that comes in the form of legislation favored by their bankrollers.

But progressive politicians have gone so far as enacting laws mandating that American children learn how to think like their special interest sponsors.

In 2009, Wisconsin Democratic Gov. Jim Doyle signed a bill mandating "labor history and collective bargaining" be taught to every public high school student in the state.

In a legislative hearing, the bill's sponsors—Sen. Dave Hansen (D-Green Bay) and Rep. Andy Jorgensen (D-Fort Atkinson)—"gave strong endorsement of returning balance to our school curricula by providing more teaching of labor in the schools," according to the Wisconsin Labor History Society website.[1]

Those guys—always thinking of the kids!

Never mind the fact that Doyle and most, if not all, of his legislative allies collected a lot of campaign money from labor unions over the years. I'm sure that had nothing to do with their desire to teach children about the virtues (never mind the sins) of the American labor movement.

The Wisconsin Labor History Society helped pass the bill and pledged to "assist teachers, school districts, parents and students in accessing materials that will provide information about union history and collective bargaining," according to the group's website.

The Society noted that the AFL-CIO and Wisconsin Education Association Council—the state's largest teachers' union—were "instrumental in attending hearings, offering testimony, making legislative contacts and doing other activities in support of the bill . . ."

Steve Cupery, president of the WLHS, said, "Once again Wisconsin leads the way in progressive labor legislation" and that "we look forward to working with the Department of Public Instruction on developing their materials for our public schools."

Are we sure we want labor apologists helping to write labor history? Shouldn't it be done by scholars who are a little more objective?

It gets even worse in other states.

In 2011, California lawmakers passed SB 48, a bill that adds "lesbian, gay, bisexual and transgender to the existing list of underrepresented cultural and ethnic groups" that should be mentioned more frequently and prominently in school textbooks and other teaching materials, according to a fact sheet distributed by the group Equality California.[2]

This is particularly important because it reverberates beyond California. Textbook manufacturers create book content to meet the requirements of large states such as California and Texas, but the same books go to states that have no such requirements. So the socio-cultural standards of California's lawmakers are adopted into textbooks in North Carolina and South Dakota.

I'm sure many level-headed people in the victimized states aren't happy about this situation. But it is what it is, and their children are forced to read what Californians want them to read.

Was the original California law even necessary?

Equality California's own fact sheet acknowledges a survey from nearly 10 years ago that indicates "many school districts already have (lesbian, gay, bisexual, transgender) inclusive curriculum and many more are interested in doing so." Eighty-three percent of districts have LGBT-related material in their "anti-bias lessons," the fact sheet said.

The guess here is that the law was passed merely to throw a bone to lawmakers' special interest friends. State Superintendent of Public Instruction Tom Torlakson issued a press release in which he said, "I applaud Governor [Jerry] Brown's decision to sign SB 48 into law, and I congratulate Senator [Mark] Leno [D-San Francisco] for authoring this important legislation. Our history is more complete when we recognize the contributions of people from all backgrounds and walks of life."[3]

Like other critics, I don't have a beef with teaching a "more complete" history—whatever that means. This legislation went beyond that. It mandated *how* it would be taught.

Southern California Public Radio reported "the measure would also require the creation of other teaching materials about sexual orientation, while prohibiting the use of those that 'reflect adversely' on gays and lesbians."[4]

This is remarkable. Would the California legislature ever pass a law making it illegal for schools to discuss Christians, white people or any other so-called privileged group in a critical manner? Assemblyman Tim Donnelly (R-San Bernardino) voiced concerns about the bill's requirement that LGBT history be portrayed positively, according to the public radio station.

"I like the idea of freedom," Donnelly said. "I think if you look at it from that point of view, that's a very different thing than saying to the entire state that 'You must teach these things, and here's how you will teach them, and how you will present them. It will be in a positive light.'"

Back to my point about textbook development. In response to Texas passing new textbook standards, California State Senator Leland Yee (D-San

Francisco), introduced SB 1451 in 2010 which began "the process of ensuring California students will not end up being taught with Texas standards," and that Texas standards had better not "creep into our textbooks."[5]

Yee then said school curriculum should be "devoid of politics." I think he really meant devoid of conservative Texas-style politics. He obviously has no trouble publishing his own left-wing agenda, considering he was a co-author of the gay history curriculum bill.

State boards of education aren't being left behind as politicians push their ideological agendas. In Maryland, the state board passed a requirement that high school graduates "prove they are 'environmentally literate.'"

"The new regulation requires districts to integrate lessons on conservation, so-called 'smart growth,' and 'the health of our natural world' into core subjects like science, social studies, math and language arts."[6]

This is not a matter of students just simply learning about these concepts—it requires them to act in a specific way. The policy states:

> "The student shall: (a) Make decisions that demonstrate understanding of natural communities and the ecological, economic, political, and social systems of human communities; and (b) Examine how their personal and collective actions affect the sustainability of these interrelated systems."[7]

Before a student is handed a high school diploma in the state of Maryland, she must conform to this policy. Or else. It continues:

> "All students shall have the opportunity to participate in the comprehensive environmental education program required by this regulation to meet their graduation requirement in environmental literacy."

This is indoctrination at its worst.

Unions and progressive activists are not the only ones trying to get their agendas in front of impressionable children. Politicians and bureaucrats have no problem jumping into the mix, as well. It really all comes down to who has the power to dictate what schools teach—and it clearly isn't the taxpayers.

CHAPTER 2

(Slanted) Social Studies Alive!

The elementary textbook "Social Studies Alive!" was thrust into the media spotlight when talk show host and author Glenn Beck became aware of the book's ideological bent. While some detractors have missed the mark by labeling the textbook "inaccurate," its real sin is its one-sidedness, which leads students to conclude that the problems identified in the book could only be solved by a powerful central government. The concerns presented in the book have merit, but the implied solutions run counter to this nation's founding principles.[8]

There is a pattern of a liberal slant throughout the book, which is written for third graders. The book identifies "community changers" who all happen to be leftists and are depicted as the good guys (and gals). No job creators or taxpayers are credited for making positive differences in the lives of Americans.

But that's not all. In the "What Are the Public Services in Our Community?" chapter, students are told, "In some countries, health care is a public service for everyone. For example, in Canada and Sweden you can see a doctor for free or for a small fee. Your community would pay the rest of the bill. Do you think health care should be a public service for everyone?"

With such a lead-in, what is the likely response from a 9-year-old? "I believe in personal responsibility, and I wonder how this would affect my parents' tax bill if America had socialized medicine?" Hardly.

Strangely, a section on child care is also included in the public services chapter.

"Child care is important, but it is not free for most people in the United States. Families have to pay for child care. It can be very expensive. Some people have to pay almost as much for child care as they earn at their jobs. Then they don't have enough money to pay for other things, such as food and health care. In some countries, child care is a public service. For example, in Denmark and Vietnam child care is free or costs very little. This makes it easier for parents to work. Do you think child care should be a public service in your community?"9

Again, what is the reasonable expectation that children will not immediately answer "yes" to this leading question? After all, what kid doesn't like "free" stuff?

The slant doesn't end there. In the "Public Transportation" section, students learn, "In some cities, you can borrow a bicycle for free. People like public bicycles. They don't cause any pollution at all! Do you think people would use public bicycles where you live?"10

In the "Whose Planet Is It, Anyway?" chapter, students learn about how terrible humans have been to Mother Earth. We've ravaged her with little regard for future generations. In the "Polluted Air" section, students read the story of a Girl Scout troop going on a camping trip and being distraught about using paper plates:

"We won't have to wash the paper plates," the girls said. "That way, we'll save water."

"There is something else to think about," said Tara's mother. "Paper is made from trees. Using paper plates means more trees have to be cut down."

"Why is that important?" asked one of the girls.

"Trees help to clean the air," Tara's mother explained. "We need trees to help fight air pollution."11

What a vexing dilemma for these youngsters. Do they needlessly waste water by washing plates, or kill trees by using paper plates? Can there be any pleasant conclusion that won't leave a 9-year-old in tears and wondering how America can be such a selfish, greedy, piggish country?

In the concluding chapter, students are asked, "How Can We Help the Global Community?" It features a drawing of a car with bumper stickers that read, "Feed the Hungry," "Think Globally Act Locally," "Save the Whales," and "My Other Car is a Bicycle." It leads one to the natural conclusion that America is somehow doing something wrong.

The section about helping the "global community" by creating economic opportunities must have been cut in the editing process. The authors likely didn't want to overwhelm children with too many new concepts all at once.

I was raised with Christian beliefs, and my wife and I are raising our children that way. While I sympathize with many of these points because of my personal beliefs (through charity, we should help those less fortunate, etc.), I have drawn the conclusion that this is little more than a one-sided book, written by progressives to lead children to certain conclusions—and believe in a government solution for everything.

I am not the only one to think along these lines. Self-described liberal *Washington Post* columnist Robert McCartney wrote "the 165-page book ... is unmistakably slanted to the left in numerous places."

After talking to parent Cindy Rose, who originally brought the book to Beck's attention, McCartney wrote, "It suggests that health care and child care should be free community services, without noting that the public must pay taxes to support those benefits."

> "... Rose was right that some passages subtly put down the United States. Page 88: 'Companies in Japan make reliable televisions and radios, German factories make some of the world's best cars. Some companies in the United States are very good at making computers.' Got that? In America, only *some* companies excel."

McCartney concluded:

> "It's risky to give third-grade students a book on the assumption that its partisan portions will be corrected elsewhere in the lesson plan. The [school district] should demand a revised version of the book or scrap it. It leans the same way I do, but a public school text shouldn't lean one way or the other."[12]

Shortly after Rose began her fight against the book in Maryland, parent Jennifer Nazlian did the same in Illinois. Nazlian contacted St. Charles Unit District 303 Superintendent Don Schlomann to voice her concerns, but he defended the text.

TribLocal reporter Melissa Jenco quoted the superintendent's review of the book:

> "Though there may be some concern about the age-appropriateness of the topics, it is the conclusion of this investigation that the textbook meets the requirements of board policy and the concerns regarding bias are a matter of opinion."[13]

Not satisfied, Nazlian appealed to the school board. She did not want the book to be banned; she was simply asked that the "other side" be presented.

That didn't save her from local *Sun-Times* columnist Jeff Ward, who used his August 1, 2011 column to ridicule Beck, Nazlian and school board member Judith McConnell:

> "When I challenged McConnell, who's a writer and editor, on this potential book ban, she said she preferred to use the word 'replace' and wrote, '. . . if I were writing history or social studies, you can be assured that what I would write would be balanced and accurate and would lean neither left nor right.'"

Ward responded by describing the book as being "balanced." He's one of a very few who could possibly believe this. But he then brought it all into perspective when he jumped issues and wrote this:

> "The truth is, when it comes to student performance, despite spending more than any other country, we're right in the middle of the educational pack. But you know what we're No. 1 in? Believing that we're No. 1 despite the evidence to the contrary."[14]

Thank you for the harsh dose of reality, Mr. Ward. Sadly, you're right. But using biased textbooks and pointing students in a particular direction to draw desired political conclusions will do little to remedy that grave problem. In fact, it's making it worse.

CHAPTER 3

Van Jones Teaches Kids about Police Brutality

In December 2010, over 1,000 New York high school and middle school students took part in the inaugural webcast of the "Speak Truth to Power" curriculum distributed by the Robert F. Kennedy Center for Justice & Human Rights and the state's teachers' union, the New York State United Teachers.[15]

According to a NYSUT blog, the curriculum "introduces general human rights issues" and "urges students to become personally involved in the protection of human rights."[16]

The web event originated from a classroom at Chestnut Ridge Middle School, which has a student population that recently scored below-average on statewide tests, according to the *New York Times*.[17]

It is extremely difficult to see how lessons focusing on corporate "greed," landmine awareness, Chinese labor camps and abolishing the death penalty will do anything to raise student test scores in math, reading and science. But I'm a knuckle-dragging simpleton, I suppose.

My favorite part of the "Speak Truth to Power" curriculum is the "Van Jones" lesson plan about police brutality. You remember ol' Van, right? He served as President Obama's "Green Jobs Czar," until it was discovered that Jones was part of the 9/11 "truther" movement, which believes the U.S. government was involved in carrying out the September 11, 2001 attacks on the World Trade Center and Pentagon.

The revelation seriously damaged Jones' reputation, so it is not unreasonable to wonder if his presence in this "Speak Truth to Power" curriculum is designed to help rehabilitate his image.

Back to the lesson plan. While the intent is supposedly to show how terrible the cops are, the first objective of the lesson is to "Know who Van Jones is and why he is a human rights defender."[18]

The lesson plan calls for students to research a state's spending on major items such as education, law enforcement, corrections and social services. The natural conclusion will be that more is spent on law enforcement than education. While we should be celebrating that it costs less to educate citizens than incarcerate them, that naturally is not the point. Far-left progressives like Jones argue that kids who receive a poor education too often end up in prison.

Therefore, the progressives want to ramp up spending for schools, which can then be squandered on giving unionized teachers free health insurance, generous pension benefits, longevity bonuses and automatic step raises. Taxpayers are asked to believe that lavishing school employee unions with all kinds of expensive goodies will somehow increase student learning, and thus, will keep more young people from a life of crime.

At the recent National Education Association representative assembly, a California delegate called for equality in prison and education spending, calling his proposal "reasonable."[19]

What does that mean in real terms? According to state statistics, in 2008, California spent roughly $47,000 per prisoner. In 2010, the state spent about $8,000 per student in its public schools. To meet the delegate's "reasonable" demand, California would need to increase school spending by $234 BILLION per year.

Sadly, even such an extravagant investment would probably do little to improve student performance, and will only end up in the pockets of unionized school employees.

The "Van Jones" lesson plan also urges students to "become a defender," and offers several ideas how to do so:

- ◆ "If there has been a specific instance of police brutality in your area, prepare materials for a teach-in at your school to inform both students and teachers about police brutality and how to work with the local police force to end it. This information can also be shared with civic and community organizations."
- ◆ "Write to the United Nations Human Rights Council citing reasons to end the abuses of law enforcement globally."
- ◆ "Research international organizations dedicated to ending police brutality and volunteer to work on their cause."

Essentially, the Jones lesson plan wants children to be automatically suspicious of the police, and look for reasons to mistrust local officers. The lesson also wants kids to think in terms of tackling issues on a global scale, which will get them accustomed to the idea that the U.N. should trump national sovereignty.

The lesson plan also cites London's *Guardian* newspaper, which responded to the police shooting of an American citizen by suggesting that the U.S. should disarm its police officers.

Guardian columnist Lola Adesioye wrote, "People in America always ask me what police officers do in the UK without guns. They find it hard to comprehend how you can enforce the law or get people to comply without the threat of a gun. I tell them I find it weird and disconcerting that police officers in the US carry guns, particularly when I hear about the various accidents that happen as a result."[20]

Perhaps the ugly riots that rocked London during the summer of 2011 will get Adesioye and other leftists to realize that if the police and private citizens are denied weapons, the only people possessing them will be the criminals, who don't abide by gun control laws.

New York parents and taxpayers ought to be very concerned that their public schools think the "Speak Truth to Power" curriculum is an appropriate use of time. Students may end up with an increased awareness of global problems, but if they don't graduate with basic academic skills, what can they possibly do about such issues?

New York schools need to focus on the rights of their students to an education that prepares them for life. Teaching the virtues of Van Jones and his agenda, particularly to students who lack basic academic skills, is a luxury that New York schools, families and taxpayers cannot afford.

CHAPTER 4

'Three Little Pigs' Slaughtered by Leftists

Leftist educators will take just about anything and turn it on its head to fit their agenda. Even children's fairy tales don't escape the slaughterhouse.

Ellen Wolpert, a longtime "early childhood educator" in Massachusetts, penned an article entitled, "Rethinking 'The Three Little Pigs.'"[21]

You're probably familiar with the story: A big, bad wolf threatens to destroy the homes of three individual pigs. There's a lot of huffing and puffing on the wolf's part, but he can only blow over the two homes that were constructed with straw and sticks.

The house left standing is made of brick, leaving readers to conclude that careful planning and hard work (as represented by the brick house) leads to success. The pigs' definition of success, of course, is to avoid being eaten by the wolf.

That's how normal, well-adjusted people interpret the story. But leftists, by and large, are dour, unhappy people who see oppression and bigotry around every corner. So it's no surprise that Wolpert sees a dark and malicious subtext to this simple fairy tale.

"I first became aware of the story's hidden messages when we were doing a unit on housing at my daycare center," Wolpert writes in the article. "As part of the unit, we talked about different homes and the many approaches to solving a basic human need: a place to live."

Having been properly "sensitized by the movement for a multicultural curriculum," Wolpert began to realize that:

"... [O]ne of the most fundamental messages of 'The Three Little Pigs' is that it belittles straw and stick homes and the 'lazy types' who build them. On the other hand, the story extols the virtues of brick homes, suggesting that they are built by serious, hardworking people and are strong enough to withstand adversity.

"Is there any coincidence that brick homes tend to be built by people in Western countries, often by those with more money? That straw homes are more common in non-European cultures, particularly Africa and Asia?"

Who knew "The Three Little Pigs" had such a hateful, Eurocentric message? I just thought the story applied to Western nations, which tend to have harsh winters and need structures made of something more durable than straw.

Perhaps Wolpert's problem is that the story glorifies hard work and initiative. Leftists have always been offended by the concept of hard working individuals doing better than their less ambitious neighbors. Where's the collectivism in that?

In any case, Wolpert offers some strategies for mitigating the damage done to children's brains by the hatefest that is "The Three Little Pigs":

"One might explain, for example, that in many tropical areas straw homes are built to take best advantage of cooling breezes. In some areas, straw homes are on stilts as protection from insects and animals or to withstand flooding.

"Such a perspective then becomes part of a broader process of helping children to understand why homes are different in different parts of the world—and that just because something is different doesn't mean it's inferior."

Wolpert doesn't seem to understand that people who build brick houses are seeking a greater level of protection—just like the people who build houses on stilts for protection from animals and floods! Forethought and protective measures are the same in any culture, regardless of what tools and materials are applied.

By why stop there? Perhaps Wolpert could revise the story so in the end, the pigs welcome the wolf, commune with him, and learn to understand why he would want to eat them. Perhaps they could dialogue with the wolf about tolerance and multiculturalism, and if they're really successful, they'll turn him into a vegan.

I'm sure the left would like to radically rework most of our cultural heritage to promote its agenda. But if they move too fast and reach too far, the people will push back. They know that. That's why they start with innocent tales like "The Three Little Pigs" and pursue their indoctrination strategy one child at a time.

CHAPTER 5

Students Chant for a Genderless Society

Any good community organizer knows an effective protest requires two things: a bad guy to attack and a catchy slogan that resonates in the public mind.

First, a bad guy must be identified. For progressives, a bad guy is anybody who disagrees with you politically, so there is no shortage of candidates. However, as Saul Alinsky's "Rules for Radicals" explains, it's best to settle on one target to isolate and attack.

Next, protestors need to come up with a snappy slogan to shout at the designated bad guy. Most people don't have the Rev. Jesse Jackson's "gift" of reducing complex ideas into simplistic rhymes, so this skill must be taught.

Which brings us to the left's answer to the age-old problem of school yard bullying. Stay with me.

The lesson is called "Gender doesn't limit you – A research-based anti-bullying program for the early grades" and it could easily be mistaken for a training manual for future union members.[22]

This charming six-part lesson plan is ostensibly designed to stamp out (mostly) gender-based bullying from Pre-K all the way through sixth grade.

Most people agree that bullying is a problem and that teachers should address it with students in a thoughtful, reasonable manner. But thought and reason are totally absent from the "Gender doesn't limit you" lesson plans, which only provide children with a designated slogan to shout at suspected bullies.

Here's an example from Lesson 4—Biased Judgments:

To start the lesson, teachers are instructed to tell students that, "Sometimes one group of kids thinks that they are better at something than another group because of their gender."

The teacher then tells students that whenever someone makes a highly offensive remark such as "boys are better at soccer than girls," they should tell the offender, "*Give it a rest. No group is best.*"

Since repetition is crucial to the learning process, the lesson plan provides teachers with four scenarios to read to students. After each one the class is instructed to shout, "*Give it a rest. No group is best.*"

Here's one of the scenarios from Lesson 4:

> (Teacher): "Paul and Vanessa are baking cookies together. Vanessa says that girls are better at baking than boys. What do we tell Vanessa? One, two, three GO!"
>
> (Class): "*Give it a rest, no group is best.*"

That's the extent of the lesson. Identify a bully (*doesn't that Vanessa sound like a monster?*), give the kids a slogan to shout, and practice with a few scenarios.

For the "Peer Exclusion" lesson, kids are instructed that "not letting someone play with you just because of their gender is called bullying . . ." Applicable slogan: "*You can't say, 'Boys/Girls can't play.'*"

For the "Role Exclusion" lesson, students are told that, "Boys and girls can have any job they want to, or do any activities that they want." If some insensitive lout attempts to define gender roles in the children's presence, they are to say, "*Not true! Gender doesn't limit you.*"

And so it goes for six lessons. Some of the remaining slogans include *"That's weird! Being boys and girls doesn't matter here"* and *"I disagree! Sexism is silly to me."*

It's obvious that these "lessons" are not designed to develop critical thought or meaningful discussions about bullying. In fact, the researchers who designed these lessons brag that "teaching students catchphrases to interrupt gender bullying" is far more effective than "using literature to challenge gender stereotypes."

Basically, this curriculum teaches kids there's a bully around every corner (in the adult world, they are called business owners) and the best way to handle him (and you just *know* it's a "him") is for the group to bully him back! It's actually a youthful lesson in union protest techniques. If the counter-bullies can outnumber and shout down the original bully, they win! Nobody learns anything about right or wrong, or how to treat others with fundamental respect, but they certainly learn the power of collective action.

In other words, strength comes in numbers, and might makes right.

Sure, the kids whose school careers are frittered away with such tripe may not be prepared to enter the competitive world of work or college. But rest assured, they will know what to do when a bully like Wisconsin Gov. Scott Walker or New Jersey Gov. Chris Christie tries to take away their collective bargaining privileges!

That's right—these lesson plans will produce some wonderful union activists someday. That's probably what they were designed for in the first place.

CHAPTER 6

Even Math Hijacked by Social Justice Activists!

Those of us who attended public schools before "social justice" infected the curriculum probably remember sitting in math class and working through problems such as this one:

> "Leroy has one quarter, one dime, one nickel, and one penny. Two of the coins are in his left pocket and the other two coins are in his right pocket. The coins have been randomly placed in the two pockets.
>
> "What is the probability that Leroy will be able to purchase a 30-cent candy bar with the two coins in his left pocket? Using the coins, explain your reasoning."[23]

We didn't know it at the time, but while we busily charted all of Leroy's different coin combinations, we were actually being taught to support America's exploitative capitalistic system.

Read the words of a "fair trade" blogger:

> "Did you know that child slavery is a common practice on cocoa farms in Ivory Coast, the world's biggest supplier of cocoa beans? Don't feel too bad if you didn't know—I didn't either until a few days ago. But now I know and so do you. I'm a huge chocoholic but now there is no enjoying a non-fair trade bar of chocolate, knowing a child may have been forced to pick the beans. There's no going back . . . Picking cocoa beans is hard and dangerous work. It takes

400 beans to produce a pound of chocolate so these kids work long and hard to get enough cocoa for even a few bars. No wonder most chocolate bars are so cheap and fair trade chocolate is so expensive."[24]

The average American "oppressor" would say that the correct answer to the sample problem posed above is, *"Leroy has a one-in-three chance of having the right combination of coins in his pocket to buy the candy bar."*

But according to the social justice crowd, the correct answer should be, *"Leroy is contributing to the oppression of the cocoa bean pickers of the world by purchasing a non-fair trade candy bar."* (Students who suggest charging Leroy with a hate crime would likely be given extra credit.)

Proponents of incorporating social justice issues into math lessons argue that to ignore the child labor that was used to help produce the candy bar is to blind students to the plight of the cocoa bean pickers. Math, therefore, is perpetuating the problem.

But don't take my word for it. Read the words of Paulo Freire, one of the pioneers of bringing social justice lessons into the classroom. Freire has said that "Washing one's hands of the conflict between the powerful and the powerless means to side with the powerful, not to be neutral."

That sentiment is echoed throughout "The Guide for Integrating Issues of Social and Economic Justice into Mathematics Curriculum," by Jonathan Osler.

In his guide, Osler writes:

> "... [T]he systemic and structural oppression of low income and people of color in the United States is worsening. The number of people in prison continues to grow, as do unemployment rates. Billions of dollars that were once available for social programs and education have been diverted to pay for war ...

"These problems and many others are being addressed by community organizations and activists, and often find their way into assignments in Social Studies and English classes. **However, in math classes around the country, perhaps the best places to study many of these issues, we continue to use curricula and models that lack any real-world, let alone socially relevant, contexts. A great opportunity to educate our young people about understanding and addressing these myriad issues continues to be squandered.**"[25] (emphasis added)

The purpose of Osler's guide is to suggest ways in which math teachers can bring social justice topics into their lesson plans.

For example, Osler suggests that a lesson about mathematical averages can be used to critique the war in Iraq. Students can "take casualty data for the past 12 months and calculate a monthly average from the perspective (of) a military recruiter and from an anti-war activist."

Instead of discussing random coins in pockets, probability lessons can be used to raise awareness of racial profiling by exploring "the probability that a traffic stop should be (and is) a person of color."

Geometry lessons can be used to "look at how many liquor stores/fast food chains are within a 1-mile radius or within 5 blocks of your schools. This can be compared with schools in other neighborhoods." Better still is a geometry lesson that tackles "environmental racism" by having students "determine the density of toxic waste facilities, factories, dumps, etc. in the neighborhood."

Lessons about war budgets, incarceration rates, AIDS cases and homelessness are also identified.

The social justice crowd knows that many Americans still cling to the antiquated notion that math teachers should stick to teaching students about math and not politics. Osler answers that criticism by arguing:

"Our classrooms are politicized spaces before we walk in the door because political parties in our country are dictating what should and should not be happening in our classrooms. What we're supposed to teach, and how we're supposed to teach it, has been predetermined by someone with a political agenda. My goal is to provide my students with varied sources of information and support them in coming to their own conclusions."

Osler isn't finished. He concedes that math can be used to help people, but argues:

"... [M]ore often it has been used to hurt them. Math was behind the development of nuclear weapons. It is used to maintain an economic divide between a handful of wealthy, white people and the billions of poor people of color around the world. It is used as a rationale for depriving people of access to cheap, life-saving drugs. So my question is: What good has the progress of mathematics as an intellectual discipline done for people? Maybe if our mathematics had a background in social justice, we wouldn't have so many people suffering around the world."

There was a time when math class existed to train the next generation of engineers and researchers. Now, math class is being used to inspire the next generation of social activists and community organizers.

That's why it's not surprising that in 2009, only 40 percent of fourth graders had math skills rated as proficient or advanced, according to the National Assessment of Educational Progress. Even worse, only 32 percent of eighth grade math students tested at those levels.[26]

Americans are continually reminded that "the world is flat," meaning our economy is so entwined with the global economy that U.S. workers are competing for jobs against workers in China, India and the rest of the world.

Despite these new realities, our public schools are promoting this silly "social justice" curriculum in math classes that should be focusing on the fundamentals. This is academic malpractice, and it is the economic equivalent of unilateral disarmament.

The laughter you hear is coming from China.

CHAPTER 7

What Would the Black Panthers Do?

The Black Panthers were founded in 1966 on Marxist principles, advocating socialism as a solution for the grievances of African-Americans.

The group quickly developed a reputation for violence and intimidation. Decades ago, members were often seen carrying shotguns throughout the city of Oakland, California. More recently, nightstick-wielding members were observed intimidating voters at a Philadelphia polling place during the 2008 presidential election.

The Panthers' "Honorary Prime Minister," Stokley Carmichael, articulated the group's radicalism in a 1966 speech:

> "This country is a nation of thieves. It stole everything it has, beginning with black people . . . This country cannot justify any longer its existence . . . I do not want to be a part of the American pie. The American pie means raping South Africa, beating Vietnam, beating South America, raping the Philippines, raping every country you've been in. I don't want any of your blood money. I don't want to be part of that system . . . That's what we are questioning, and whether or not we want this country to continue being the wealthiest country in the world at the price of raping everybody else across the world . . ."[27]

The far-left Southern Poverty Law Center, which also has curricula featured in this book, has labeled the New Black Panthers a "hate group." That's saying something.

But that's of little relevance to "educators" like Wayne Au, a Seattle high school teacher-turned-professor.

Just to appreciate how far on the fringe Au is, consider what he told SocialistWorker.org about standardized testing.

"Test makers purposefully choose to use questions on tests that rich kids will usually answer more correctly than poor kids," Au said. [28]

Throughout his teaching career, Au has taught his students to apply the principles of the Black Panthers to their own problems. Seriously.

Au writes:

> "I taught about the Panthers in the context of a high school African Studies class in Seattle that focused on African history and the experience of Diaspora. Of the 30 working- and middle-class students, most of them 10th graders, 25 were African American, four were white, and one was Chicana. When I teach about the Black Power Movement, I try to connect the movement to today's issues. One way is by having students review the Black Panther's Ten Point Program and develop their own personal versions of the program."[29]

Au highlights several students' Panther-inspired Ten Point Programs for their own lives. One student offered general demands, such as "free housing for the homeless people in the United States" and "non-racist presidents." Another student developed a list for the "Gay/Lesbian/Bisexual/ Transgendered/and Questioning Community."

Another student, "Marcus," goes straight for the jugular and "challenges capitalism and corporate control of the United States." Here are a few of his ideas:

+ We want the mask of capitalism lifted and economic classes disbanded.

- We want an end to the solitary control of mass media by corporations.
- We want an end to the health insurance system in America. It is time to end corporate control of Americans' health.
- We want fair treatment of all criminals. Rich money launderers and tax fraud offenders should receive the same punishment as armed robbers and drug dealers.
- We want an end to all corporate funding of education. The public education system is being used by corporations as a training ground for future employees.
- We demand an end to the growing separation of the economic classes of America. The enslavement of the middle and lower classes by the bourgeoisie must be put to a stop.[30]

Au finds this "piece notable for its relentless attack on corporate America; it demonstrates a growing consciousness among students about issues such as sweatshops, media bias, campaign financing, and the encroachment of private industry on public education."

There are many more incredible comments in Au's lesson plan, but perhaps the most revealing is when Au laments that more students didn't strike a more radical pose:

> "My hope is that the lesson **laid a groundwork**, so that in the future the students will have some tools with which they can assess issues they see in their own communities and their lives and perhaps develop Ten Point Programs of their own. The Ten Point Program may be a place where students are able to find their voice and speak out about the problems they see in this world—and, more difficult, begin to **organize** to put their program into practice." (emphasis added)

Incredible. A more fitting title for Au's lesson plan would be "What Would the Black Panthers Do?" because apparently in Au's eyes, they are to be held up as freedom fighters and not the violent thugs they were, and continue to be.

CHAPTER 8

The Slaveholders in Your Wallet

Every year around the Fourth of July, we read news stories about the ignorance of American students in regard to U.S. history.

In June 2011, the *New York Times* ran a typical story, titled "U.S. Students Remain Poor at History, Tests Show." Here's the opening paragraph:

What does this say about our teachers?

"American students are less proficient in their nation's history than in any other subject, according to results of a nationwide test released on Tuesday, with most fourth graders unable to say why Abraham Lincoln was an important figure and few high school seniors able to identify China as the North Korean ally that fought American troops during the Korean War."[31]

A few days later, well-respected historian and best-selling author David McCullough was asked in an interview why our public schools do such a terrible job teaching history. McCullough reasoned that teachers may be graduating college unprepared to competently teach history. He also faulted "boring" textbooks that are "so politically correct as to be comic."[32]

McCullough's explanations contain a measure of truth, but there is another, more sinister explanation for our historic amnesia: *It is being created by design.*

Like most patriots, McCullough argues that "History is a source of strength. It sets higher standards for all of us."[33]

But compare that with the views of the social justice crowd, as articulated by Oregon high school social studies teacher Bill Bigelow:

> "Schools are identity factories. They teach students who 'we' are. And as [progressive historian] Howard Zinn points out . . . too often the curricular 'we' are the great slaveholders, plunderers, imperialists, and captains of industry of yesteryear.
>
> "Thus when we teach about the genocide Columbus launched against the Taínos, or Washington's scorched-earth war on the Iroquois, or even Abraham Lincoln's promise in his first inaugural address to support a constitutional amendment making slavery permanent in Southern states, some students may experience this new information as a personal loss. In part . . . this is because they've been denied a more honorable past with which to identify—one that acknowledges racism and exploitation, but also highlights courageous initiatives for social equality and justice."[34]

Bigelow's quote comes from "Rethinking Our Classrooms: Teaching for Equity and Justice, Volume 2," and is indicative of the new approach many teachers are taking into the classroom.

In another "Rethinking Our Classrooms" article, the aforementioned Howard Zinn writes:

> "Granted, it is good to have historical figures we can admire and emulate. But why hold up as models the 55 rich white men who drafted the Constitution as a way of establishing a government that would protect the interests of their class—slaveholders, merchants, bondholders, land speculators?"[35]

Can you believe the nerve of those 55 rich, white bastards? How dare they create a society where it's possible for free people to work hard, acquire wealth and build influence within their communities, regardless of their social status at birth?

Zinn urges a rewriting of the history books to eliminate the oppressors and to honor the champions of equality and justice. He proposes replacing "slave-owner" and "killer of Indians" Andrew Jackson with John Ross, "a Cherokee chief who resisted the dispossession of his people, and whose wife died on the Trail of Tears."

He wants Teddy Roosevelt banished from history textbooks for "his militarism, his racism (and) his love of war." Zinn even proposes removing Roosevelt from Mount Rushmore and replacing him with author Mark Twain, an outspoken critic of TR's warmongering.

He goes on to lambast Woodrow Wilson and JFK for their militarism, too, and wonders:

> "Should we not replace the portraits of our Presidents, which too often take up all the space on our classroom walls, with the likenesses of grassroots heroes like Fannie Lou Hamer, the Mississippi sharecropper? Mrs. Hamer was evicted from her farm and tortured in prison after she joined the Civil Rights Movement, but she became an eloquent voice for freedom."

Zinn is conducting a clever sleight of hand. By promoting people such as Hamer, he and his fellow progressives give the impression that American history is being gently rewritten only to give more attention to freedom's most "eloquent" voices.

That's rubbish.

Think about it. Progressives pride themselves in not seeing the world in simplistic terms of "right" or "wrong." In fact, these are the same people who like to remind us that one person's "terrorist" is another's "freedom fighter." Progressives relish nuance. They wallow in it. And now these same people want to demonize Teddy Roosevelt and Abraham Lincoln?

Zinn was a knowledgeable guy. He knew full well that Teddy Roosevelt was not an intractable racist. In fact, segregationists were mortified when TR dined with civil rights leader Booker T. Washington in the White

House—during his first month in office! Doesn't Roosevelt deserve a little love from the social justice crowd for that alone?

And Abraham Lincoln's early views on slavery may have been wobbly, but he is rightly remembered as the Great Emancipator. Zinn also knew that Lincoln met with abolitionist Frederick Douglass in the White House after delivering his second inaugural address. Isn't that more significant than what Lincoln said during his first days in office?

The truth is that progressives want to discredit standard American history as much as possible, while bringing singular attention to American figures who fought for collectivism and the redistribution of wealth.

The progressives know that to kill a tree, one must sever it from its roots. That's why they are busy scrubbing textbooks and school curricula of references to our founding principles and the so-called "slaveholders in our wallets." Leftists know it will take a historically-illiterate generation of citizens to allow them to remake the country in their collectivist image.

CHAPTER 9

The 'Collective' American Revolution

There's nothing progressives love more than a revolution.

But they strongly prefer social revolutions—you know, the type where the starving masses rise up with pitchforks and overthrow the money-grubbing ruling class.

That clearly wasn't the nature of the American Revolution. But facts don't stop at least one liberal revisionist from creating his own flawed portrayal of the American fight for independence. Instead of giving due credit to the Founding Fathers, who were clearly the driving figures behind our break with Great Britain, author Ray Raphael argues that independence came through the efforts of "people who had learned the power of collaborative effort."

In his article "Re-examining the Revolution," Raphael argues that schoolchildren should be taught that the war was driven by angry masses who rose up and worked together to defeat an oppressive monarch.

Raphael writes:

> "The democratic nature of our nation's creation is hidden from view by stories fashioned in a different mold. Individual heroics trump collective action; the few take the place of the many. Both real history and the meaning of American democracy are lost in translation . . . Our texts are based on warmed-over tales of the 19th century such as Patrick Henry's 'Liberty or Death' speech . . . and 'Paul

Revere's Ride.' Although many historians know better, these stories work so well that they must still be included, regardless of authenticity or merit."[36]

Raphael seems particularly agitated by the credit traditionally given to the leaders of the revolution.

". . . George Washington, Benjamin Franklin, Thomas Jefferson—we speak of these illustrious *individuals as the Revolutionaries, even as we proclaim they are special, not like the others.* These people are then called 'leaders'; all others become mere followers . . . The famous Founders, we are told, made the American Revolution. They dreamt up the ideas, spoke and wrote incessantly, and finally convinced others to follow their lead. But in trickle-down history, as in trickle-down economics, the concerns of the people at the bottom are supposed to be addressed by mysterious processes that cannot be delineated."

This is an odd point for Raphael to argue, because leftists make historical heroes out of individuals all the time. One of the left's folk heroes is the founder of the United Farm Workers, Caesar Chavez. Numerous lesson plans praise his leadership in organizing boycotts and unionizing farm workers; he was the leader, they were the followers. How is that different from the texts that highlight the actions of the American founders?

In any case, Raphael sums up his point by arguing "the United States was founded not by isolated acts of heroism but by the concerted revolutionary activities of people who had learned the power of collaborative effort."

Of course there's some truth to that. No successful war has ever been fought without a great deal of cooperation between thousands of command officers and foot soldiers.

But the soldiers only took to the fields at the prompting of the leaders of the Revolution. And most of the leaders were wealthy people who were spoiling for a fight with King George III for their own selfish reasons.

Our revolution was purely political, with one group of economic elites (wealthy American colonists) breaking away from a historically dominant group of economic elites (the wealthy British ruling class) in a manner consistent with a mature child breaking away from parents. Leaders such as Thomas Paine and Samuel Adams used angry propaganda to inspire many Americans into providing the manpower necessary to prosecute the war, but they did not frame it as some sort of collective social movement. To borrow Raphael's words, "the concerns of the people at the bottom" were never a consideration. This was not the French Revolution.

In fact, a significant portion of the general population remained loyal to the British crown throughout the war, and many were hostile to the new republic that formed after the war.

Luckily, the rabble-rousers from the American elite class—like Paine and Adams—were successful in prompting enough average people to support their cause to form an army and achieve an unlikely victory.

It can be argued, however, that the masses clearly profited from the American Revolution, at least in later generations.

The Founding Fathers provided us with the blueprint for a society that allows the common people to design their own government and direct its actions. The wealthy few who led the effort to gain independence from Britain created a unique society that allows financial and social mobility for the masses. The founders are indeed the heroes of the common person, because they created a free society where average people can be heard and have their grievances addressed.

That freedom allowed popular movements to take hold in later centuries and improve American society. Without the environment of personal liberty and political freedom created by the founders, the abolitionist movement, the organized labor movement and the civil rights movement may well have been crushed by oppressive regimes operating without the restraints of the Constitution (which was written by the founders).

Raphael is dead wrong. Our Founding Fathers were indeed individual geniuses who (arguably) picked a fight with Britain, sold their countrymen on the idea of independence, and created a society that allowed for the eventual participation and heroism of the masses.

Raphael may want to paint the American Revolution as an earlier version of the Soviet, Chinese or Cuban revolutions, but it was no such thing. Reasonable (adult) students of history know that.

The danger is having left-wing revisionist historians sell their phony version to wide-eyed American students while we are not watching. As Raphael himself admitted, "History, like politics, is based on framing and spin."

CHAPTER 10

Students Fight 'Racist Cookies' with 'Self Love Strudels'

In my opinion, Ted Kefalinos is an idiot.

Kefalinos is the Greenwich Village baker who created "Drunken Negro Head" cookies, supposedly to honor Barack Obama's inauguration.

Unsurprisingly, the cookies weren't a hit. But Kefalinos got his comeuppance. New York City *Fox* reporter Arnold Diaz produced an unnecessarily long four-and-a-half minute story—a lifetime in TV news—just to show how big of a boob Kefalinos is.[37]

Most 10-year-olds can recognize blatant racism when they encounter it, and know how wrong it is. But social justice teachers in the Big Apple saw an opportunity to teach kids the ins and outs of social activism. Not only did they help organize protests outside Kefalinos' bakery, Lafayette French Pastry, but they created lesson plans to hammer the point home. Yes, they produced lesson plans covering five days of class time to dwell on this non-issue.

The lessons, published by Bree Picower of the Education for Liberation Network, are geared toward upper elementary students.[38] The lessons require students to watch both the aforementioned TV news story and the teachers' YouTube videos of the protests. Students then engage "in a discussion on their reactions and compare/contrast the activists' responses in both situations."

The activist teachers go on to compare the Kefalinos kerfuffle to the Greensboro, South Carolina sit-ins of the 1960s, when activists occupied

Woolworth's lunch counters to protest the chain's segregation policies. Seriously.

In "Unit 3: Taking Action for a Yummy Cause," students "explore the issue of social injustice through an incident that happened in their own backyard. They will work collaboratively to engage with their fellow community members as they address the issue and share knowledge with others." To accomplish this, the lesson calls for students to write letters of complaint to the Better Business Bureau, organize a town hall meeting, and interview neighbors to see what they think.

Another lesson calls for students to create their own Public Service Announcement to say "No More Racist Cookies!"

But the best lesson is saved for last as students get to fight back against this baker's racist cookies by baking their own social justice creations. Deeming it a "peaceful protest," students hold a bake sale in front of Kefalinos' shop and sell items such as the "Self Love Strudel" (unlikely this is a shout-out to former Surgeon General Joycelyn Elders), "Tolerance Tart," "Equality Éclair," and a "Diversity Doughnut."

WNYC reports the drop-out rate in New York City is 16 percent but, by God, those kids will know how to make a delicious "Social Action Shortcake" before they leave school.[39]

The only way this lesson could have been worthwhile is if it had been used to illustrate the necessity of one of America's most precious liberties—freedom of speech—regardless of how unpopular the speech may be.

A true educator would remind students that while Kefalinos is a moron, he has an absolute right to be a moron. Students would have received a real lesson in American democracy if they had been encouraged to march outside of the bakery, defending Kefalinos' right to speak his mind and bake any sort of political cookies he cares to. The students would have learned that in America, we don't have to agree with someone's words or opinions to defend their right to speak or publish them. It's freedom of speech that has given birth to our greatest social movements. The American Civil Liberties

Union, a very liberal organization, fights every day for the right of people to say what's on their minds, even if it's offensive garbage.

But alas, the progressive educators missed another chance to teach children a truly useful lesson about our nation and Constitution. Instead they wasted the opportunity on yet another pointless exercise in political correctness.

CHAPTER 11

'Planning to Change the World'

Many teachers' contracts require educators to keep a planning book.[40] But there's no reason for the books to be boring, lifeless creations that only contain pages and pages of blank calendars. The New York Collective of Radical Educators has come up with a useful purpose for those books in the "2011-2012 Planning to Change the World—A Plan Book for Social Justice Teachers!"

The introduction states that the book is "designed to help teachers translate their vision of a just education into concrete classroom activities . . . This plan book was created to make that job just a little easier by helping you turn your daily lesson planning into a strategy for teaching toward democracy, equity, fairness and peace."[41]

Each planning page includes dates for social justice conferences, social justice birthdays and historic events, a quote of the week, and a suggested question teachers "can use to start a discussion with your students."

For each month, historical events are noted, such as August 5th, which represents the "30th anniversary of Ronald Reagan breaking the air traffic controllers union." Or August 10th, which is "the 50th anniversary of the U.S. spraying toxic herbicides in Vietnam." September 21st is notable as the "International Day of Peace," while February 17th is notable for being the birthday of Black Panther party founder Huey Newton.

Other red letter days include:

- November 20: Transgender Day of Remembrance
- November 26: Buy Nothing Day

- December 16: Religious Freedom Day
- April 29: 20ᵗʰ anniversary of the start of the 1992 Los Angeles "uprising"
- May 1: International Worker's Day/May Day
- May 20: 110ᵗʰ anniversary of Cuba's independence from U.S. occupation
- May 28: 120ᵗʰ anniversary of the founding of the Sierra Club

The book identifies resources for students to learn more about Islam, Kwanzaa, Hinduism, Buddhism and Sikhism. Apparently Christianity and Judaism are too mainstream for the social justice activists, and are not included in the book.

Ironically, one of the questions for students to ponder is, "How do you think schools should handle religious holidays?" Others include:

- "Why do Americans take loving care of cats and dogs, but eat cows and chickens?"
- "How does the existence of HIV affect the decisions you make in your daily life?"
- "What is the best type of economic system to ensure human rights for all?"
- "What do you think the Americas would be like if they had never been colonized by the Europeans?"
- "Who should be responsible for ensuring that businesses adhere to safety standards? How should the government respond when they don't?"

Perhaps the best question is, "If you knew child workers made your favorite candy, would you still buy it?" Oh, the decisions!

The planning book also highlights a quotation from the aforementioned Huey Newton, who said, "The policemen or soldiers are only a gun in the establishment's hand. They make the racist secure in his racism."

The book quotes "civil rights activist" Yuri Kochiyama as saying, "History, depending on how it is told, can be used as a weapon to divide us further or as a vehicle to seek truths that might bring us to greater mutual understanding."

In the NYCoRE plan book, Kochiyama is pictured wearing a "Free Mumia Abu-Jamal" t-shirt. Mumia was convicted of assassinating Philadelphia police officer Daniel Faulkner—execution-style—in 1982. Despite folk-hero status on the left and several legal appeals, he's sentenced to rot in prison. He, too, was a member of the Black Panthers.

Other quotes include, "Another world is not only possible, she is on her way. On a quiet day, I can hear her breathing," by Arundhati Roy; or "We see the rebirth of this culture, the dance and music, as the best treatment, the best medicine for young people to find their identity and their self-esteem," by Vernon Bellecourt.

Before the radicals can indoctrinate students, they have to indoctrinate teachers. And there are still many teachers who don't currently subscribe to the theory that public education should be used to create a new generation of leftist revolutionaries.

The goal is to slowly win over the skeptical teachers, through the publication of "planning books" and other materials full of radical spew. The suggestion to teachers (many of whom are as politically naïve as their students) is that they should really care about this stuff, and have a responsibility to share it with their students. If they can convince teachers to do that, they are more than halfway home.

Chapter 12

'F is for Fair!'

I have two sons; the oldest one is in his first year of traditional schooling. Both of them have picked up a habit that has really gotten under my skin: When I say "no" to a request—or demand—their response will be, "That's not fair."

Curious as to where they picked up this retort, I ask them what that means. They can't define it. It just seems to them like something you say when you don't get your way.

They will eventually learn that life is not fair.

That's one of the most valuable lessons children can learn. They should be taught to make the best use of the resources available to them and rely on their own intelligence and determination. If they wait around for life to be completely fair, they will be waiting a long time—and in a state of desperate poverty.

Someone will always come from a wealthier family that can afford tuition at better schools. Someone will always be a little bit smarter or a little more driven. Someone will always have personal connections that allow them special access to the best schools or the most desirable companies. You don't waste time whining about the advantages others have. The trick is to focus on what you want and plow through the obstacles until you get it. That's the American way.

But progressive "educators" don't see things that way. They don't recognize the great personal rewards (material gains as well as self confidence and self-esteem) that derive from hard work and perseverance against all odds. To them, the only issue is creating an absolutely level playing field for everyone from birth, which is an absolute impossibility.

That fact didn't stop them from creating "F is for Fair!" which is another lesson plan from the Southern Poverty Law Center's "Teaching Tolerance" series.[42] The sole purpose of this little beauty is to teach kids the basics of envy and class warfare, nothing more ... and certainly nothing less.

The lesson accomplishes this by asking kids to "evaluate how well the world is doing when it comes to providing a free, equal, quality education to our youth." Don't let the word "evaluate" fool you into thinking that there is something vaguely academic going on here. There's not. In this lesson, "evaluate" simply means to look at another with covetous eyes.

The lesson begins by having students define "what 'equal' or 'fair' means to them." No talk of how the dictionary defines those words or how they have been interpreted throughout American history (such as Americans traditionally supporting equal opportunities, but not necessarily equal outcomes). Instead, each child is essentially asked to say how they *feel* about fairness and equality.

Next, teachers are told "to foster emotion" in students by giving them a few examples of gross injustice.

Here's scenario #1: *"East Side Elementary school received a new playground this year; North Side Elementary did not."*

Scenario #2: *"Ms. Cook's class got new computers; Ms. Young's class got their old ones."*

Teachers are then told to ask students "if these examples are fair." Of course, neither scenario provides enough information to make any kind of an informed decision. For example, maybe North Side Elementary doesn't need a new playground because its current one is quite good. Or maybe Ms. Young's class doesn't need new computers because her students only use them for word processing, whereas Ms. Cook's class needs computers that can handle the new math software.

If the students are really on the ball, maybe they'll ask some of these questions, but critical thought isn't the point of the lesson. Rather, its purpose is to sensitize kids to the inequality that's all around them, and to breed jealousy.

This dopey, half-baked lesson concludes by having students create an acrostic poem based on the word "fair." (The lesson plan provides an example: "F: *Fair means the same*; A: *All children should have an education*; I: *I am happy I have a good school*; R: *Real kids deserve a real education*.")

Teachers are then instructed to:

> ". . . [P]ush the concepts of fair and equal resources in school a little further by dividing the kids into two groups. Group A should be given a wide variety of new art supplies to decorate their acrostic poems. Group B should only be given old, broken crayons and pencils to decorate their poems. As students begin to complain, they are sure to use phrases like, 'But that isn't fair!' Use this as an opportunity to drive home your point about equal resources."

A truly valuable lesson in this context would be for the kids with the broken crayons and pencils to outwork and outsmart the more privileged group, so their finished products are just as good or better, despite the inferior condition of their tools.

But the point of this progressive lesson, I'm afraid, is to teach the kids with the broken crayons that they should cry and protest about the unfairness of it all, until authorities address their grievances. Or worse, that students should go and seize the superior supplies from the "haves."

Students who have the misfortune of participating in such asinine lessons will learn the real meaning of "unfair" when they leave school and are unable to secure a decent job or entry into a good college. They might wonder how "fair" it was that their teachers were more concerned about pushing a social justice agenda than they were about teaching the fundamentals.

On the other hand, knowing how to write acrostic poems about fairness might take them quite far in the ranks of community organizers.

CHAPTER 13

Students Psychoanalyze Halloween Costumes

Never mind that many modern students are functionally illiterate or unprepared for higher education. Social justice teachers believe there are bigger things to worry about—such as interpreting what Halloween costumes say to us.

That's why they have developed a lesson plan which "is designed to help students look critically at the Halloween costumes marketed to them." Those last three words are key. Once again the idea is to teach children that evil corporations are the problem.

Published by the Southern Poverty Law Center, "What Do Halloween Costumes Say?" can also "be used to develop guidelines for acceptable holiday garb," according to its authors.[43]

Students are required to browse catalogues and analyze the costumes to determine if they are promoting a specific consumer brand, violence, militarism, or certain racial and gender roles.

Students then report on the costumes to the whole class, with a volunteer keeping notes on a chart. Students then explain "patterns" that emerge from their findings.

Students are then told to take the next steps:

- Brainstorm a list of ways to identify stereotypes represented in Halloween costumes.

+ Pledge to think about this list in selecting costumes to wear at school or at home.
+ Write a letter to parents sharing what the class learned and asking for their support.

But the fun doesn't end there. Math and "social justice" components can be added as well.

> "Students can apply basic concepts of statistics and data analysis by selecting methods to represent and describe patterns revealed in the class-generated chart. For example, students might select pie charts as a way to display a disproportionate representation of male models in violent costumes."

To strike back against stereotypical costumes with the sword of social justice, the lesson suggests "the class can write letters to the editor of local newspapers, expanding their sphere of influence beyond their own school, and/or to the catalogue publisher."

If American students were kicking butt academically, there might be downtime for this silliness. Tragically, they are not. But rather than spending classroom time catching up to their global peers, they're looking for hidden messages in Halloween costumes and the way they're supposedly marketed.

The true masquerade in this lesson plan involves progressives dressing up as educators and pushing this type of trash.

SAVE THE WHALES BY KILLING
CAPITALISM

The first goal and primary function of the U.S. public school is not to educate good people, but good citizens. It is the function which we call—in enemy nations—"state indoctrination."

—Jonathan Kozol

CHAPTER 14

Green Curricula's Real Target is the Free Market, Not Global Warming

Back in 2008, *Detroit News* columnist and WJR talk radio personality Frank Beckmann brought to light a series of lesson plans produced by Creative Change Educational Solutions, a non-profit outfit that produces classroom materials for teachers who want to instruct their students on environmental issues.[1]

Beckmann decried the fact that the Creative Change environmental curriculum focuses on criticizing capitalism by having students compare "wages and working conditions in factories in China and Vietnam (to) corporate profits . . . and compensation for chief executive officers." In other words, the distribution of wealth is unacceptable and must be changed. That will save the whales!

Laughable as it may be, this type of "environmental lesson" has spread throughout southeast Michigan. One school district, Bloomfield Hills—which ironically serves one of the wealthiest communities in the state—purchased the curriculum for $750.[2] Ann Arbor Public Schools paid $4,900 for a day-long seminar.[3] Similarly, Eastern Michigan University paid Creative Change $19,133.67 between 2007 and 2008 to "identify community groups and schools, help to develop, plan for, and facilitate stakeholders meetings, and collaborate writing the implementation proposal."[4]

Eastern Michigan University, Bloomfield Hills schools and Ann Arbor schools spent our tax dollars to spread this poison around the region.

There's nothing wrong with teaching kids to turn off the lights and if it's yellow let it mellow. But Creative Change goes beyond common sense reforms and pushes a progressive socio/political agenda.

One sample lesson plan—"Economics for the Common Good"—focuses on the Gross Domestic Product (GDP) as a misleading indicator of economic "progress."[5] You see, if there is an oil spill, millions—if not billions—are spent cleaning it up. That looks good for the GDP but not so good for the environment, according to their theory. So the progressives sought to compensate for that by devising the "Genuine Progress Indicator" (GPI). This measurement would take into account the "bad things" that grow the GDP to reflect the "actual" progress society is making.

"There is a growing acknowledgement that the GDP does not reflect sustainability's aim to balance economic concerns with environmental and social goals," the curriculum states. But the alternative "GPI measures our combined economic, social, and environmental progress."

The writers say this is a great idea because, for instance, bees will be able to get long-overdue credit for their contribution to society:

> "The GDP also ignores the many life-sustaining services performed by nature, such as pollination by bees and water purification by wetlands. Scientists conservatively estimate that these services are worth about $33 trillion per year, almost twice the total world GDP of $18 trillion."

How a scientist can calculate the value of chemical-capturing mud is beyond me. And I'm not sure what the point is. Governments at all levels have passed many laws protecting even the smallest of wetland areas, and I haven't noticed bees being added to the endangered species list.

Are we expected to somehow compensate the bees and plants for their trouble?

One challenge for the writers of the lesson plan was making all of this nonsense understandable for pimply-faced teens. The "Economics for the

Common Good" lesson suggests creating a cartoon from an absurdly cynical perspective.

> "... Create a comic strip featuring the adventures of a (Gross Domestic Product) superhero and super-villain. The superhero, for example, would drive a gas-guzzling SUV, crash it into a lake (causing an expensive clean-up), rack up huge hospital bills, and file a lawsuit. The villain, on the other hand, wouldn't even have a car, would walk to work, and resolve conflict through discussion and mediation."

These silly characterizations will help the students get the point. At least the radical, uncompromising point that the authors want them to get.

It's no wonder America's future is looking more bleak, when this is the type of garbage filling our students' minds. Instead of belittling free markets and economic success with ridiculous dramatizations, perhaps it would behoove teachers to reflect on the real progress, innovation and high standard of living that capitalism has brought to America.

Perhaps the message would be more legitimate if progressives would acknowledge that our wildly successful economic system can continue to exist while making room for common-sense environmental protections. They are not mutually exclusive. But that would mean admitting that it's possible to own a car, work hard and earn an advanced salary, while still caring about the bees and the trees.

That, of course, would not be consistent with the socialist agenda. The real targets of the Green Movement are free markets and capitalism, not theoretical man-made global warming. It's pretty clear that the one-sided "lesson plan" offered by Creative Change is brown and should be flushed down.

CHAPTER 15

The Story of Annie Leonard's Socialism

A series of left-wing, anti-capitalist videos have been racking up millions of hits on YouTube, thanks in part to public school teachers and university professors who have adopted them into their lesson plans.

The most prominent of the videos is "The Story of Stuff." According to a 2009 front page article in the *New York Times*, "over 7,000 American schools have ordered the DVD."[6]

"The Story of Stuff" was created by socialist and Greenpeace activist Annie Leonard. "Stuff" disparages America's consumer society and attacks capitalism, or as Leonard calls it, "the *current* economic model."

"Stuff" was funded by the mysterious Tides Foundation—a left-wing, big money group that also funded the Association of Community Organizations for Reform Now (ACORN) before the organization's corruption became an embarrassment to the left and it rotted away.

There has been a successful effort to debunk Leonard's indoctrination scheme, including well-directed criticism from the Heritage Foundation (heritage.org). According to Heritage's Rory Cooper:

> "'The Story of Stuff' highlights the very extreme left's Greenpeace view of America. Essentially it tells the story of how America is not a nation to be proud of, and in fact, your child should be ashamed for living in it."[7]

Cooper quotes Leonard as saying:

"Let's start with the government. Now my friends tell me I should use a tank to symbolize the government and that's true in many countries, and increasingly in our own. After all, more than 50% of our federal tax money is now going to our military."

Cooper responded by writing, "Aside from throwing a little jab towards the expense our government spares to its ultimate duty of protecting us, and telling children to resent our armed forces, it is also factually inaccurate. The Congressional Budget Office estimated direct defense outlays to be roughly 20 percent (of spending) in Fiscal Year 2007 . . . ," which is the year the video was produced.

But Leonard's own words show that this "Story of Stuff" project is simply a means to an end. The end, of course, is to transform America's economy from a free market system to something that can only be described as socialism.

"I go around the country and I show the 'Story of Stuff' film and for those of you that have seen it you know it lays out a pretty broad, pretty systemic critique of the economy—of the **current economic model**," Leonard said in a May 2010 speech in South Carolina.[8] (emphasis added)

The problem is Leonard, and many like her, don't have the courage to simply say they want to ditch capitalism. Instead, they use poll-tested phrases like "an economy that works for everyone." Or, she objects to "trashing each other on the equity front," and apparently believes "stuff" should be distributed evenly.

"We're not sharing the stuff we use well enough," she says.

What Annie Leonard—and many others with socialist beliefs—lack is the courage to say what they would do about it. Clearly their remedy is more government intervention in our lives. More regulation, more taxes, more nudges—or outright shoves—to get us to act as they would see fit.

They don't say that because such honest words would provoke stiff opposition. So they go about it in a different way, using propaganda to turn students against free markets. Consider one of Leonard's analogies from the May 2010 speech:

> "I'm looking forward to the day that I show the 'Story of Stuff' film and someone asks from the audience not 'what can I buy differently?' but 'what meaningful collective action can we take to solve this problem at its root, to build a healthy, sustainable, equitable and fulfilling economy?'"

So she wants to replace the individual consumer mindset with a "collective" one. Just makes you want to travel on over to Haight-Ashbury and get your smoke on, doesn't it?

Leonard continues:

> "I'm not saying we shouldn't shop responsibly when we do shop—of course, of course—we should buy the least toxic, least exploitative product available, of course. But our power is not in perfecting our skills at choosing the least hazardous thing on the menu. The real power lies in choosing what's on the menu and the only way to do that . . . is to reengage our citizen and community self to build a different kind of economy **so that the only choices available to everybody are the safe and healthy choices** . . ." (emphasis added)

This is the problem with Leonard and her propaganda. She wants government to protect us *from ourselves*. While she is clever in leaving us a few choices, her form of government would narrow the list to very little choice at all. It's broccoli or cauliflower, not broccoli or French fries. After all, Big Brother knows best!

Leonard's philosophy is killing America, which was once the greatest hope on earth. The socialist mindset is continuing to creep into our government and society. And government schools give the progressives a platform every time they show "The Story of Stuff" to students.

Even with such a compliant public education system, Leonard isn't happy:

> "The second thing that I've learned since releasing the 'Story of Stuff' film that has me worried is the intensity of the effort to silence this conversation. While the response to 'Story of Stuff' has been overwhelmingly positive, there are some people who make up for the smallness in their numbers and in their thinking by their disproportionate access to TV talk shows—who want to marginalize, threaten and silence people who are speaking up for a fundamentally different economic model ... not business as usual with a little recycling, but something **fundamentally different**." (emphasis added)

Those who believe in free markets very much want to have this conversation, Ms. Leonard. We'd just like you to be open about your goals. Share your transformative "solutions" so we can debate them—as adults. And leave the children out of this debate.

I'd love an example—just one—to support Leonard's claim that a TV talk show host has tried to "silence" her. Unlike those on the left, conservatives believe in everyone's right to free expression, even if we disagree with what we hear. That's the America we're trying to protect from the progressives.

So what remains to be seen is if Greenpeace, Tides and other left-wing organizations will be successful in their quest to transform America into a nation that fits Leonard's description:

> "I cannot tell you how often someone raises their hand after watching this pretty broad critique, and says, 'What can I buy differently to solve this problem?' Or they say, 'What can I do?' And I want to know where people are and so I say, 'What can you think of to do?' And almost entirely, at meeting after meeting after meeting, what I hear are individual and consumer responses: I can recycle, I can ride my bike, I can change my light bulbs, I can stop drinking bottled water, I can buy organic, all of these things. Now, of course, those are all good things and of course we should all do those things but those aren't about making systemic political and economic change. To me, those things fall in

the category of being a responsible adult, like you floss your teeth and you make your bed and you recycle and that's what you do if you're a responsible adult—it's like household management. That's not economic and political transformation which we so deeply need."

The success of "The Story of Stuff" has prompted Leonard to expand beyond so-called environmental issues, which underscores the fact that her agenda goes far beyond ocean levels and the anatomy of a landfill. She has since created "The Story of Citizens United v. FEC," which deals with corporate political spending. Leonard's other popular propaganda videos include "The Story of Electronics," "The Story of Cosmetics," as well as "The Story of Subsidies."

This is perhaps the most dangerous lesson analyzed in this book. Parents need to be aware because Leonard's work (and comparable efforts) have become ingrained in countless schools. The Carroll County school district in North Carolina lists "The Story of Stuff" as a lesson for its third graders.[9] Similarly, Frederick Douglass Elementary School in Cincinnati, Ohio "liked" "The Story of Stuff" on its Facebook page. TT Minor Elementary School in Seattle featured a link on its website's menu bar directly to "The Story of Stuff's" site.[10]

On *Current TV's* website (*Current TV* is owned by Al Gore), "marisa bklyn" commented on a brief article featuring Leonard's video. The author's poor grammar has been corrected:

> "I'm an elementary school teacher and I've shown 'The Story of Stuff' to some of my students. My class has discussed the ideas brought up in this film. I like that it could be brought down to the level young kids can understand. Forget about high school. I think it's important to teach kids about consumerism, recycling, and wastefulness at a young age. Don't wait till high school."[11]

Don't dismiss Leonard's agenda as unachievable. It's having its desired effect. *The New York Times* article quoted a nine-year-old boy as pondering whether or not a new set of Legos "would be bad for the planet."

Leonard has every right to say and create whatever she wants to. But how long will we allow public schools to be used to peddle Leonard's "economic and political transformation" philosophy? Is your child's school promoting this sort of political agenda? Put this book down and find out. Now.

CHAPTER 16

'I Pledge Allegiance to the Earth'

With America's public schools continuing to slouch towards globalism and progressivism, it's just not cool to say the Pledge Allegiance to the (American) Flag anymore. Now, more and more students are pledging allegiance to the Earth. There are actually several variations, but here are two:

- "I pledge allegiance to the Earth and all the life which it supports. One planet in our care, irreplaceable, with sustenance and respect for all."
- "I Pledge Allegiance to the Earth and to the Flora, Fauna, and human Life that it Supports, the Planet Indivisible with Safe Air, Water and Soil, Economic Justice, Equal Rights and Peace for All."

This phenomenon was exposed by Glenn Beck, who shared a poster featuring the Earth pledge on his *Fox News* show. It was sent in by a viewer who found it displayed at the front of her second grader's classroom.

This Earth pledge has actually been around for quite some time. One of the earliest references is from 2001, when, two-and-a-half weeks after the September 11 terrorist attacks, a Los Angeles City Council member, Ruth Galanter, proposed reciting it before every council meeting.

Galanter, along with six other council members, wanted to say a variation of the Pledge to the Earth after the Pledge of Allegiance. "Galanter said she first heard the pledge used at school in Westchester, and that it is used by many schoolchildren in Los Angeles," a September 27, *Daily News of Los Angeles* article noted.[12]

71

Later that year, a spokeswoman for Galanter said the councilwoman's intent was to "elevate the council's thoughts to global harmony" and that, "the pledge would give credence to children's hopes and beliefs that if we work together, we can accomplish a better world."[13]

More recently, White Oaks School in California's San Carlos district celebrated Earth Day by having students create a "pledge tree," according to a June 2010 PTA newsletter. One student wrote, "We pledge allegiance to the Earth, and all the animals and plants on it."[14]

Not to be outdone, former Maine high school art teacher Rosalie Tyler Paul wrote a commentary in *The Times Record* in which she called for America to reject the idea of nationalism and "acknowledge that the Earth is our home."

> "So while we go on loving our own bed and our own community and the larger and larger spaces around us, we can see that the nation is not the parcel most in need of our loyalty and allegiance. Fortunately, the purpose and courage we need can be found better in Earth citizenship than in nationalism."[15]

The leftists continually predict calamity for the environment, knowing that is the surest way of emasculating countries of their national sovereignty and empowering progressive global institutions to "solve" such problems. After all, the environment does not stop at a nation's borders.

The global warming alarmists are today's version of the "useful idiots," a term popularly attributed to Soviet dictator Vladimir Lenin. He was referring to Americans who did the Soviet Union's bidding during the Cold War. The "useful idiots" were giving credibility to one of the 20th century's most prolific killers, all the while believing they were acting in the interest of humanity.

Today's American leftists who continually slam their country over trumped up environmental concerns can certainly be put in the same category. I'm sure Venezuelan strongman Hugo Chavez appreciates Americans like Tyler Paul.

The One World environmentalists naively believe that if America were to become no more powerful than a third world country, and if we were to offer emission concessions to nations like China and India, that somehow the environment will be saved. It is a dangerous, reckless ideology that is spreading into our schools, through such seemingly harmless items like the Pledge to the Earth.

Just consider Paul's ending to see for yourself:

> "So here's to a celebration of our Earth on April 22 and to all that day helps us to understand. Let us pledge our allegiance to the Earth and agree that our actions will consider her health as vital to our own health, that we will honor our interdependence with each other and with all species of life.

> "Let us mark the day by flying the Earth flag from every flagpole—at every school, every town office, every public building. At the end of the day let us not take them down but let them fly on as a symbol of a new understanding of our place in the complexity of Life."

The present day Lenins must be smiling as the new generation of "useful idiots" destroys America from within, all in the name of saving the environment.

CHAPTER 17

When Kids Resist Global Warming Indoctrination: One Teacher's Story

On July 30, 2011, a few thousand teachers' union activists descended upon Washington D.C. for a "Save Our Schools" rally. The keynote speaker that day was actor Matt Damon, who took the occasion to bash standardized testing—you know, virtually the only thing we have at our disposal to assess student achievement and promote teacher accountability.

"I said before that I had incredible teachers," Damon told the crowd. "And that's true. But it's more than that. My teachers were EMPOWERED to teach me. Their time wasn't taken up with a bunch of test prep—this silly drill-and-kill nonsense that any serious person knows doesn't promote real learning."[16]

He added that teachers should help kids fall "in love with the process of learning" rather than worrying that students are filling "in the right bubble on a test." Damon, a proud leftist, was repeating an oft-heard criticism that standardized testing harms student learning. They argue that "teaching to the test" creates student automatons who are only capable of regurgitating factoids deemed important by the government.

Many Americans reason that if a test covers the essential things kids need to know, then "teaching to the test" makes total sense. They wonder what all the fuss is about.

Frankly, I wondered that myself—until I came across an article titled, "Teaching About Global Warming in Truck Country." It was written by Jana Dean, an eighth grade science and social studies teacher in Washington state.[17]

In the article, Dean recounts the difficulty she had in selling students on the dangers of man-made global warming. Dean teaches in a rural community where most families use trucks in their everyday activities. Early on in the global warming unit, one student asked if Dean was telling him he could never drive a truck like his father does.

Dean writes:

> ". . . When Alex first crossed his arms, I began to realize that indicting our beloved motors for global warming before building a ton of background would be like petting a cat in the wrong direction. At the same time, it was a sign that I was going in the right direction: Change doesn't happen without resistance . . . **My upfront commitment to action** had activated in my students a fear of losing a way of life they'd been raised to inherit . . . I decided to carefully sidestep any mention of the causes of global warming until we thoroughly understood the effects." (emphasis added)

In order to sufficiently scare the children, she used a curriculum developed by the Union of Concerned Scientists that links global warming to floods, droughts, heat waves, wildfires—basically anything weather-related. Then students learned how global warming is melting the polar ice caps and causing an increase in malaria and other diseases in tropical Africa.

Believing she had sufficiently primed the pump, Dean then "asked students to write about what concerned them most about global warming. As they shared aloud, I wrote down their worries on poster paper hung at the front of the class. The mood was somber. My students sat so still and silent we could hear each other swallow."

"I thought that by then we might have been ready to look again at the causes of climate change," Dean writes.

But instead of reaching for a science textbook, she reached for a video produced by Greenpeace that "bombards (viewers) with a message about our cars, our trucks, our factories, our consumption." The film did not go over very well:

"As he put his notebook away, Ron slammed it shut and said, '*I don't get it. What are we gonna do? Stop driving?'* Consternation ran through the class. '*What about my quad . . . my motorcycle . . . how will we get to school . . . too far to ride my bike.'* I had no answer."

Dean "spent the next two weeks building science background," which amounted to having students learn about greenhouse gases and how the manufacturing industry spews more of those compounds into the atmosphere with every product it makes. Dean writes:

"By the end of the period they saw greenhouse gases everywhere—in tailpipes of tractors, in stockyards, in the power behind the pump, in oil wells, in the manufacturing of hydraulic fluid, in the coal that powered the cement kiln."

Like a good propagandist, Dean issued a call to action to her students, instructing them to find ways they could "combat global warming" within their families, their school, their country and the world at large. The class identified a variety of possible actions, from taking shorter showers to urging the passage of international treaties "to decrease dependence on fossil fuels."

The lesson culminated with a recycling program Dean's class established for the school.

"But the recycling project helped my middle school students see . . . how the actions we take collectively speak much louder than words. And I want my students to see themselves as agents in our world, rather than subject to it. They made a change in their school that will last much longer than their short stay in 8th grade. **And they've established a climate of concern in their school that I can take further next year.**" (emphasis added)

Not only has Dean crossed the line that separates teaching from propagandizing, but she spent almost a month's worth of class time on her global warming unit, with the grand result being a few recycling bins placed around the school and a "climate of concern" among students.

It is doubtful that Washington state's standardized test asks students to explain how owning a truck contributes to global warming. That means in a nine-month school year, Dean only has eight months to teach the rest of the 8th grade science curriculum—the stuff that kids will actually be tested on.

It is clear that "teaching to the test" leaves less time for social engineering lesson plans, which cramps the propagandists' style in a major way.

Here's how one social justice educator summed it up:

> "Teachers who are pressured to teach towards an exam, or to teach from a textbook that their school district has chosen, find it very difficult to try anything non-traditional in their classrooms for fear of reprisal from their administration and concern that their students won't pass high-stakes tests."[18]

Parents and taxpayers want kids to leave school with the knowledge and skills that will allow them to succeed in life. That stands in contrast to the progressives' goal of creating a generation of good global citizens who are equipped to identify and combat the suffering supposedly caused by capitalism, which they believe is the driving force behind most of the world's greed, inequality and pollution.

Standardized tests are designed to measure math and reading skills, but they cannot measure a student's commitment to social justice or disdain of the free market system. Suddenly the left's hatred of standardized testing makes sense, doesn't it?

CHAPTER 18

Walmart Sucks!

Back before citizen journalist James O'Keefe exposed the abject corruption of the Association of Community Organizations for Reform Now (ACORN) in 2009, the group was a major political force for the progressives. And ACORN's then-CEO Bertha Lewis was a powerful political player, until the scandal brought the good times—and government funding—to a screeching halt.

But Lewis hasn't allowed public embarrassment keep her down. On May Day 2011, Lewis appeared before the nutty Church of Earthaluja in New York City. Lewis' part of the "service" was to besmirch Walmart, and she didn't disappoint the faithful. Her diatribe against the retail giant was so stirring that it ended with a congregation-wide chant of *"Walmart sucks! Walmart sucks!"*[19]

Lewis is just one in a long line of leftists who routinely smear Walmart, which happens to be America's largest employer. In fact, the anti-Walmart campaign is so popular that it is even being waged in many of our public schools.

In 2005, the Ecology Center of Berkeley, California created a school lesson plan entitled, "Big Box Stores," which reviewed all the supposed downsides to all-in-one stores with low prices. But it doesn't focus on Lowes, Home Depot, Target, Costco or the like. Nope—just Walmart.

The lesson plan introduces the subject to students by saying:

> "...Walmart scours the planet for the best discounts: About
> 70 percent of the items sold in Walmart stores come from

China, where many workers make an average of 64 cents an hour. American workers make, on average, less at Walmart than at comparable jobs and have fewer health benefits and no access to union organizing."[20]

The lesson plan doesn't provide a single example of anyone being forced to work at Walmart, either in America or in its product-producing factories elsewhere. Furthermore, Walmart employees, like all other workers in America, have access to union organizing. The unions are just too lazy to organize them, and individual employees who have tried have repeatedly been rebuffed by their colleagues.

And to top it off, can you believe those bastards have the gall to deliver goods at low prices? How dare they!

Anyway, the first step in the lesson requires students to write freely about how Walmart makes them feel. Students then share their feelings with the class. Under the heading "Walmart," one student writes the responses on the board.

Then, the class answers questions such as:

- ♦ "Is Walmart good for the U.S.?"
- ♦ "Is making money more important than the environment or civil rights?"
- ♦ "Does the bottom line ensure the safety of the environment and civil rights?"

Clearly, with the way the lesson is slanted, the natural answer to these questions is "no." God help the student (and his grade) who answers "yes."

Next, students engage in a "town hall meeting" where each is assigned the role of either a local business owner, a parent in a low-income working family, an unemployed person, or an environmentalist. Students then need to research their positions on such websites as walmartfacts.com, sierraclub. org, americanprogress.org, alternet.org and religioustolerance.org. (The last site directs students to an article that criticizes Walmart for supposedly refusing to stock the "morning after" abortion pill.)

Needless to say, none of these web sites begin to touch on the positive aspects of the retail chain. But based on the one-sided information they cull from the websites, students get to decide whether or not to let Walmart into their community, which, of course, is not how it works in a republic. But who needs to point that out when there's propaganda to be poured into childrens' minds?

Then the students read a quote from the ubiquitous Van Jones:

> "One of the problems right now is you've got a bunch of white folks who get it, and have moved on to being vegan and trying to have solar powered hair dryers, or whatever. But what about the person living 20 minutes away who's happy that Walmart might give them access to commodities they don't have to take four buses to get to, and who would be happy getting a job anywhere, even [if] it was smoking up the sky a little bit?"[21]

In other words, some of us are just too dumb or selfish to hate Walmart. The students' next task is to "design a public relations campaign for the environmental movement."

> "Now we need a new slogan, one which addresses the problems Van Jones described . . . What should it be? Create your own one-sentence slogan . . .

> "Keeping Van Jones' comments in mind, write the script for a 30-second TV or radio ad which describes your new and improved environmental philosophy."

This statement crystallizes the intent of this and many of the lessons: Nudging students into thinking a certain way, without presenting them with all sides and letting them draw conclusions for themselves. Teachers using these lesson plans are determined to shape student thinking to their liking. The point is not promoting freedom of thought but molding beliefs into a desired ideological direction. Radical teachers hate Walmart, and they are going to make sure their students hate it, too.

CHAPTER 19

Are You An 'Environmental Racist'?

The Southern Poverty Law Center is at the forefront of pushing the social justice curriculum into our schools. One series of SPLC's lesson plans is designed to introduce students to the concept of "environmental racism," which claims that minorities are subjected to harmful materials at a disproportionate rate.

While there may be some truth to that observation, left-wing radicals stretch it to the limit, with observations like "the operations of the Environmental Protection Agency and other federal and state agencies have had discriminatory impacts on communities of color."

You don't have to stick your nose very deep into this hole to get a whiff of the real goal—another attempt at financial reparations, through a radical redistribution of American wealth. And the purveyors of this philosophy want to drive it home by driving it into our children's brains.

"Introducing Kids to the Idea of Environmental Racism" is the title of one of the SPLC lessons. The objective is for students to "explore the concept of environmental racism through their own experience of fairness."[22] This is done by giving all students a piece of candy to eat, while forcing only some of the students to keep all of the wrappers. The lesson, I guess, is that some unfairly bear the brunt of environmental hazards.

Variations of the word "fair" are used throughout the lesson. "For younger children, linking the concept of environmental racism to their own understanding of fairness will help them grasp the injustice of this practice," it reads. This summarizes the intent of the lessons.

Van Jones, the one-time White House "Green Jobs Czar," is a huge believer in the existence of environmental racism. And for him, it's clear the concept is a vehicle to obtain more socialistic goals, whereas the lesson plans are more nebulous. Jones explained his views to the far-left *Mother Jones* magazine:

> "Environmental justice is the movement to ensure that no community suffers disproportionate environmental burdens or goes without enjoying fair environmental benefits ... It's the environmental racism that allowed for powerful people in society to turn a blind eye for decades to the downsides of the industrial system that got us to this point. So there's a direct relationship between environmental racism and the lack of sustainability of society as a whole. We were the canaries in the coal mines."[23]

Conjuring up environmental racism is a way to accomplish the real objective: a redistribution of wealth. Jones continues:

> "Before, it was much stronger on demanding equal protection from environmental bad. Now we are also demanding equal opportunity and equal access to environmental good . . . We want an equal share, an equitable share, of the work, wealth and the benefits of the transition to a green economy."

With school teachers introducing these concepts into society through children, the goal is to create a sense that there is a problem that requires a government solution. Jones offers some potential answers:

> "There's going to be a lot of jobs weatherizing buildings, putting up solar panels, manufacturing parts for wind turbines and wind towers. All that's work, and we want to make sure that the green economy is an equal-opportunity, diverse economy that can lift millions of people out of poverty."

In other words, eradicating "environmental racism" means creating multi-billion dollar public works projects, and placing them in communities chosen by the left. Rest assured, these government funded jobs will likely end up in union-friendly locales; Right-to-Work states need not apply.

While Jones works on that mission, the foundation is being laid by teachers across America who employ the "environmental racism" lesson plan.

Lessons based on candy wrappers are pretty weak, even by the left's standards. So teachers are told to dress the lessons up by incorporating arts and communications components. For example, students may have to evaluate news reporting on environmental racism. "By creating a mock news broadcast to cover an instance of environmental racism, your students will build understanding of the news values that shape media coverage, while exploring the concept of environmental justice," the lesson reads.

Notice how the lesson quickly moves beyond the mere concept of environmental racism to treating it as pure fact. Notice also that students are compelled to do something about it.

It reads:

> "Tell students to script and create a mock television news report on their example of environmental racism. One person should be assigned to play the reporter, and the other three should play the 'sources'—fictitious people who provide additional insight on the problem."

'Fictitious' sources? Was this lesson written by former *CBS News* anchorman Dan Rather?

While the issue of minorities (and lower-income people) being subjected to harmful materials is legitimate, the lesson plans lead students to the shaky conclusion that the problem is intentional and that Jones' solution, quoted below, is the correct one:

> "I just say cap, collect, and invest . . . We just want to make sure the money comes in and is invested in people and not just handed right back to the polluters . . . We are going to have steps and stages here. The first step is going from just

grey, dirty suicidal capitalism that doesn't even try to take account of any sustainability at all to a form of capitalism that does."

In other words, students are taught that the solution to the problem is the creation of government-funded industries. It's a clever way for radicals like Jones to redistribute America's wealth, while helping out their friends in the unions. It's obvious that "Green Jobs" is just the left's euphemism for central planning and crony socialism.

CHAPTER 20

Were Your Vegetables 'Picked by Union Farm Workers'?

In a school lesson plan published by the California Federation of Teachers, fourth grade students learn about the life of a tomato, or at least the observations of one rather progressive-minded, fictional tomato plant. It's called, quite creatively, "I, Tomato."[24]

The story is dedicated to the "farm workers of America, by whose hands we are all fed." There's no mention of the farmer who invested a great deal of money purchasing the land and equipment necessary to create the farm, not to mention the jobs on the farm. But that's understandable, considering that the lesson plan came from one of the nation's more radical teachers unions.

"Everybody knows that tomato plants can't really talk," the book begins, "but if they could, they might say something like this . . ."

The tomato plant goes on to talk about how it got its start in a hothouse, and was eventually moved to a growing field. While telling the readers its life story, the tomato plant includes a loving tribute to the nursery workers (Juana, Dolores and Rajib) to whom "I owe my life," as well as the field workers who tenderly cared for the plant while it grew to maturation. (The tomato plant gives a special shout out to field worker Connie whose "warm hands . . . carefully placed me in the ground.") This is one very thoughtful tomato plant.

The drama of the story revolves around the tomato plant's sickness, which was triggered by its move from the comfort of the hothouse to the harsh realities of the growing field.

Wait a minute. Are we supposed to feel sorry for the farm workers or the tomato plants? Read on:

> "The next day I was sick, and I stayed sick for a day or two. In those early bad times, the thing that got me through was 'plantstory.' Right, plantstory. I had heard some guy in the nursery telling a bunch of kids the story of the tomato . . .'Tomatoes don't give up,' I remembered him saying."

Wow. Who knew tomato plants or their offspring were so inspiringly resilient? Still, danger lurks everywhere for vulnerable fruits that are popularly (and mistakenly) considered vegetables:

> "I have to tell you some of the bad stuff, too. Bugs! These little white things came by one day and started to attack me. They started eating my branches and taking water out of me. Marcos came by with this spray and shot me right in the face with this horrible dust. It stuck on me and made me sick. The bugs were gone, though, and didn't come back. But I heard about some places where they dump the poison cloud out of a flying machine, every week or something, on us and the people who are working. It kills the bugs all right, but it poisons everything else, like the people and the water and the land."

So we finally get to the environmental part of the lesson. I knew it had to be hidden in there somewhere.

Still, a key purpose of "I, Tomato" is to make sure the schoolchildren know precisely who to thank for their ketchup and salsa. (Hint: It's the people who do the jobs Americans are supposedly unwilling to do—and the union they belong to.)

The tomato plant concludes its story:

> "I want to thank the farm workers who helped me in my career: Juana, Dolores and Rajib; Finoy and Carlos,

Connie, Lupe, Marcos and José Manuel, who took my tomatoes to you. It is to them I owe my life and you owe your tomatoes."

Again, no appreciation for the owner of the land that gave life to Mr. Tomato Plant.

Should children know where fruits and vegetables come from? Yes. Should they know farms are an integral part of an economy where people work hard to provide for their families and are an asset to society? Of course.

It's even proper to make them aware of the debate surrounding the use of agricultural pesticides, as long as they hear both the pros and cons of the discussion.

But none of that is the main point of the story. It turns out to be a promo for the United Farm Workers. Why else would the last question in the story deal with a subject that wasn't brought up in the entire lesson?

"Many farm workers belong to a union. Do you know what a union is? If you were a worker, would you want to belong to a union? How can you find out if your fruits and vegetables were picked by union farm workers?"

"I, Tomato" is a perfect example of unionists using public school class time to introduce children to their particular school of thought. It offers nothing that will help students prepare for (a non-union) life. But that was never the goal of the lesson plan, was it?

UNIONS CULTIVATE SOLIDARITY
IN THE CLASSROOM

*Education is a weapon, whose effect depends on who
holds it in his hands and at whom it is aimed.*
—Joseph Stalin

CHAPTER 21

'Organizing' the Curriculum

It's no secret that the organized labor movement has been on the decline for decades, both in terms of membership and in public support for the cause.

So Big Labor has been going out of its way to sow the seeds of rebirth for the movement, in the hope that the upcoming generation will believe organized confrontation is the natural and necessary approach for employees in any line of work.

Sadly, thousands of radical union teachers have been more than happy to incorporate those ideas into everyday lesson plans.

The Education and Labor Collaborative, managed by New York-based Adelphi University, states that "labor would benefit from a better-educated public, one that understands and supports the role of trade unionism in a democracy," according to its website.

> "Imagine how much easier and effective the work of unionists would be if a generation of children of working families graduated from high school with an understanding of their right and duty to be heard, the power of joining together in a common cause . . .

> "Educators, in collaboration with unionists, can break the cycle of reproducing the economic structure through schooling, and change the cultural climate that denigrates poor and working families."[1]

"Break the cycle of reproducing the economic structure?" Does that mean getting students to turn away from the time-tested concepts of free markets and capitalism?

An entire book, "Organizing the Curriculum," edited by Rob Linné, Leigh Benin and Adrienne Sosin, gives teachers ideas on how to weave union history and perspective into lesson plans.

In the introduction, Linné explains:

> ". . . The long period of self-censorship among educators regarding class and labor issues may no longer hold. We cannot claim to be teaching for social justice if we ignore the class warfare being waged all around us. In recent decades we have witnessed another great redistribution of wealth upwards that at last seems to be shifting attitudes and making the argument that identity, rather than class, should be our central focus of interrogation more and more out of touch with reality . . .

> ". . . Bringing labor into the arena of K-12 education will undoubtedly meet political resistance, but an increasing number of educators are motivated to take up the challenge . . . We have also found that allies working in the labor movement as well as colleagues in the field of labor studies are similarly enthusiastic about our project. It is because of this solidarity that we hold out hope that the subject of labor, which has been so effectively silenced as a subject for learning, can at last be openly explored in classrooms across the country. As we go about the work of organizing educators around this project, we are inspired by, and are learning from, our friends in the labor movement. This school reform project is a part of a larger movement for social reform in which organized labor is now playing a leading role."[2]

This part is critical: Teaching labor history and tactics helps progressives develop a base of new union activists who will seek to alter American culture.

"Social reform" they call it. It is not just about teaching their particular version of American history. It's also about training students to carry out the radical mission that is implanted in their brains.

Linné writes:

> "This is necessary because curriculum materials alone are insufficient to enhance students' understandings about the nature of society or to inspire activism among youth. We advocate collaborations with unionists and community activists as a means of making learning relevant to young people."

"Labor Matters," a lesson plan developed by the Southern Poverty Law Center, states that its purpose is to "help (students) understand the importance of the labor movement."[3]

Objectives include:

- Students will understand their connection to the history of organized labor.
- Students will identify major strategies and tactics of labor organizers.
- Students will consider ways to apply these and other tactics to improve working conditions today.

Pointy-headed union apologists want the kiddies to appreciate the role of organized labor—at least from their one-sided perspective. And the Southern Poverty Law Center is enthusiastically answering the call.

CHAPTER 22

'Click Clack Moo'—Teachers Who Indoctrinate

A children's book the AFL-CIO says teaches a "valuable union lesson" is likely being read to children in your local public school.[4] "Click Clack Moo: Cows That Type" tells the story of unhappy cows that refuse to work until the farmer meets their demands. The cows complain to the farmer that they are cold, and ask for electric blankets. When the farmer refuses, the chickens—in a bold act of solidarity—refuse to lay eggs until the cows get their way.

The story seems innocent enough. I found it on my own kids' bookshelf after my wife bought it at a garage sale. I read half of it before I realized it was union propaganda.

Leftists have developed several lesson plans that get the story in front of children, ensuring that "Click Clack Moo" is not just a book sitting on the shelf.

One lesson plan, written by Mary Eggebraaten, calls for students to read the book and learn four new vocabulary words: *union, strike, laborer* and *negotiate.*[5] They then re-read the book and think of the story in those terms, lest the kids think this is just a fun little story about a cow whose hooves can miraculously peck typewriter keys.

Students then write their own version of "Click Clack Moo" and must incorporate those same four terms. They then read their version to fellow students who mark *union, strike, laborer* and *negotiate* off a check list when they hear the words.

Finding another way to get the book in front of children, Texas (yes, Texas) teacher Michelle Anthony wrote the lesson plan "Click Clack Moo: Electric Blanket Science."[6] Students read the story and then compare electric blankets with regular blankets, presumably to meet science application requirements. Seriously. The lesson reads:

> "Objective: To compare and show differences/similarities in a regular blanket vs. an electric blanket and have kids determine why the cows and hens requested the electric blankets in the story . . .

> "Strategy and procedure: Read the story and have children offer their predictions as to why they think the cows and hens requested an electric blanket, rather than a regular blanket. Then plug in an electric blanket and have children observe how the temperature change warms the blanket. Let students feel the warmth of a regular blanket and compare it to the warmth generated by the electric blanket. Discuss the difference and review their predictions."

The book and related lesson plans are not limited to an audience of second-graders, those old fogies. A Chicago preschool teacher, Kati Gilson, told her students—again, preschoolers—about her "regular trips to Madison to protest" Wisconsin Gov. Scott Walker and his collective bargaining reform proposal, according to an article published in the June 2011 edition of *Chicago Union Teacher*, the magazine of the Chicago Teachers Union.[7]

Then Gilson had an epiphany: "Click Clack Moo" is about unions and collective bargaining!

> "Before the lesson, my students knew that they loved learning, their teachers and their school. They couldn't connect strikes and protests with their education. However, even our youngest children can understand decent working conditions and wages if presented in a way they can understand. This book teaches them these concepts using a fun plot and rhyme.

"The story led to lively debates. I was able to incorporate vocabulary words like *strike, collective bargaining* and *negotiate* with my preschoolers. I showed them that these actions are happening in their backyards by showing them pictures from Madison . . ."

Again, these are preschoolers being taught about strikes and collective bargaining. Why waste time on colors and letters? Let's get to the stuff that really matters: union power!

"My preschoolers understand what a protest march is and why it is important. As we gear up for what looks like a big battle it is important for us to teach our children and families why we are taking a stand. We will need their support just as they need ours."

That's the point—building support for the union agenda. And it's delivered to gullible children under the guise of a disgruntled cow using a typewriter.

Chapter 23

Kindergarteners of America Unite!

In typical union and socialist propaganda, employers are depicted as cruel and uncaring business owners who never miss an opportunity to cheat and mistreat workers.

Big Labor's "us versus them" worldview is so entrenched that there's no recognition of the fact that the vast majority of successful companies value their employees, and do whatever they can to retain their best workers. That reality, of course, undercuts the relevance of unions.

So what's a union to do?

Like their fellow travelers in the "man-made" global warming community, the unions know they have to indoctrinate the young with their propaganda. But when you're dealing with kindergarteners, you have to insert the concept of unionizing subtly into lessons. You'll get blank stares if you talk about the virtues of Jimmy Hoffa or the Service Employees International Union.

The California Federation of Teachers produced the perfect solution with the lesson plan, "Trouble in the Hen House: A Puppet Show."[8] To spare you the unpleasantness of reading this bilge, here's the basic plot: A bunch of hens feel "oppressed" by the farmer, so they band together and create Hens United. The angry unionized chickens are too powerful a force for the farmer to handle, so he capitulates to the hens' demands. Here's a key excerpt:

> **Henrietta** (the hen): Farmer Brown, we have something to say. This is what we chickens want:

1. More and better food. No mold, no sand in our corn.
2. Freedom to walk around outside and a bigger hen house.
3. Each hen will lay an average of four eggs a week.
4. Stop punishing us. Let Hortensia come back.

Farmer: No way! Who ever heard of chickens telling the farmer what to do? Shut up and get back to the henhouse!

Chickens: No, Farmer Brown, not this time! And besides those things, you have to recognize our union, Hens United, or we'll all stop laying eggs!

Farmer: OK, OK, if I have no eggs to sell, I'll go bankrupt. We'd all starve, so I guess I'll have to do what you say. Since you're all together, what can I do?

Chickens: We won! We stuck together and we won! *Si, Se puede.**

With this puppet show, educators now have a way of teaching children how to use mob tactics to get what they want from those in positions of power. This puppet show fits very nicely into a kindergartener's school day—right after finger painting and just ahead of snack time.

Lest readers are tempted to dismiss this as some wacky lesson plan that's never applied in an actual classroom, consider this story from the 2009 California Federation of Teachers convention:

> ". . . Bill Morgan uses a short puppet show, *Trouble in the Hen House*, to teach about the strength and value of organizing unions. His students act out a story about hens who organize a union to fight against unfair compensation and poor working conditions. Through this activity, the students learn about becoming activists, organizers, negotiators and problem solvers."[9]

Just to remind you, the "students" the newsletter is referring to are kindergarteners and first graders.

With labor activists starting to propagandize students in kindergarten, they'll already be brainwashed by the time they learn to actually think critically. Vladamir Lenin is quoted as saying, "Give me four years to teach the children and the seed I have sown will never be uprooted."

The scary part is that this is happening so early in children's lives and little if anything is being done about it.

Note: "Si, Se puede" is Spanish for *"Yes, it is possible,"* but is sometimes translated as *"Yes, we can."* Where have I heard that before?

CHAPTER 24

Wisconsin Teachers Conscript Students into Big Labor's Budget Battle

Some public school teachers are very serious about their union affiliation. Sometimes it seems they're more interested in that than they are in teaching the basics.

And there are many teachers who are not shy about bringing their union political agenda into the classroom. They believe it's their duty to familiarize young children with the organized labor concept, and their right to brainwash children about specific union issues.

That's what they've been taught to do by the leading "thinkers" of the labor movement, who are quoted extensively in many university schools of education. Consider the words of leftist historian Howard Zinn:

> "If teacher unions want to be strong and well-supported, it's essential that they not only be teacher-unionists but teachers of unionism. We need to create a generation of students who support teachers and the movement of teachers for their rights."[10]

Kate Lyman, a teacher in the Madison, Wisconsin school district, has clearly heard that call.

She was among the thousands of Wisconsin teachers who abandoned their students in February, 2011 to participate in public employee union protests at the state capitol building. They were upset by new legislation limiting teachers' collective bargaining privileges. The mass absenteeism forced the Madison district to close for several school days.

But Lyman was not satisfied with simply protesting. When she returned to school, she decided it was necessary to make sure her students understood the union point of view. Never mind the fact that thousands of Wisconsin residents agreed with the state's move to adjust collective bargaining, due to the unions' stubborn refusal to make temporary concessions to help cash-strapped schools.

For Lyman, there was only one point of view—the union's. And that's all her students heard. She shared her classroom indoctrination experience in an article she penned for *Rethinking Schools* magazine.[11]

At first Lyman, who already has a warning in her personnel file for violating the school's "controversial issues" policy, claimed she simply invited students to share their personal observations of the recent protests.

One student opined that Walker would "send (illegal immigrants) back to Mexico." Lyman apparently didn't correct this idiotic notion. Another said, "Does he want to be rich?" "Yeah, he wants to be rich!" Then there were the assorted "He's selfish," "He's crazy," "He's guilty," "He's greedy," and, "He should go to jail, even though he's governor."

I'm pretty sure Lyman was pleased with their responses, and with her successful effort to transplant her own thoughts into their minds.

Then she went even further. She created math problems with attendance statistics from the protests. She had her student teacher create a PowerPoint presentation, with side-by-side pictures of the Madison protests and images from the 1960s civil rights showdowns in the south.

Lyman writes:

> "I hesitated to ask this last question as the students were examining a photo of white segregationists ('We want a white school!') juxtaposed to a Walker supporter ('WisSCOTTsin'). But we talked extensively about rights, in the context of both the Civil Rights Movement and the Capitol protests."[12]

I'll bet you can't guess how old these kids were. Surely if they were tuned into the news, and were aware of the protests, they must be high schoolers. Wrong. Lyman was warping the brains of 2nd- and 3rd-graders.

I have a hard time believing Wisconsin taxpayers would agree with this strategy. They pay taxes so children will be taught the fundamentals of learning. They do not pay to send the kids to leftist indoctrination camps.

The superintendent of Madison schools should make sure Lyman understands that point, once and for all.

Then there's the case of Dale Weiss, a third-grade teacher in Milwaukee Public Schools.

Like many of her colleagues, Weiss was upset by pending budget cuts in the district. Her knee-jerk reaction to the situation was for the school board to cough up more money to avoid layoffs. It never occurred to her (or her union leadership) that the teachers could sacrifice a few perks from their collective bargaining agreement to keep a few colleagues employed. They simply wanted the school board to magically produce more money.

Weiss decided to lure her students into the fight. She recently recounted her experience in a piece for *Rethinking Schools*:

> "Right as the bell was about to ring at the end of the school day, I casually mentioned to my students that I wanted to learn more about doing art with children since Ms. Sue [the art teacher] would not be with us next year. The students clearly were taken off guard: 'But I thought if we wrote letters to the school board there would be more money for MPS and we could keep Ms. Sue.'"[13]

So the students eagerly prepared letters, innocently assuming their teacher was telling them the whole truth about the situation. Two students were chosen to read their letters at a school board meeting.

> "Michael and Dakota read their letters at that meeting, and they asked for more money for our school. I really

thought we would get more money. But now I don't think it happened.

"Looking at the disappointment on their faces, I realized I had unintentionally led my students to conclude that if we believed something to be unfair and took action, the unfair situation would turn into a fair one. I remembered saying over and over: 'There is always something you can do to try to turn the unfair situation into a fair one.'

"Yet my students heard something quite different. In their hope and optimism as 8- and 9-year-old children, they knew that their actions would bring about a miracle. My heart sank; I felt I had let my students down."

Yet there was a silver lining to the experience for Weiss.

"The process of addressing budget cuts with my students taught me an incredible amount," Weiss wrote. "I learned that laying a social justice foundation for young students is a complex process. I learned when issues are addressed, they need to be revisited many, many times."

I'm certain the president of her union was proud. I'm not so sure parents would feel the same way, if they understood what was happening in her classroom.

For Lyman, Weiss and other unionists, the students are little more than political pawns in their game. They're setting them up to do their dirty lobbying work.

This is Social Justice Indoctrination 101. This is not teaching 3rd graders to read, write and compute basic math (not to mention appreciate America and its importance to world history). This is enlisting them in the Big Education army to do the bidding of the adult union members who want Viagra insurance coverage maintained, even if it means axing the school librarian.[14]

It's immoral for school teachers to brainwash young students in their political philosophies. If they were true educators, they would present all sides of an issue (if third graders could understand the complexities of school budgets and spending) and let them draw their own conclusions.

CHAPTER 25

Students Form (Unionized) 'Yummy' Pizza Company

The California Federation of Teachers thinks it's important for kids to learn how to run a business. I come from a small business family, so I'm cool with that.

However, the CFT-produced "The Yummy Pizza Company" lesson plan immediately starts off on the wrong foot. Why? Because it's not delivered from the perspective of an entrepreneur, but rather a disgruntled employee.

This lesson is part of CFT's "Labor Studies Curriculum for Elementary Schools." Several other lessons from the union-produced curriculum are discussed throughout this book.

"The Yummy Pizza Company" is a series of 10 lessons, which take up to 20 classroom hours over a two-week period.[15] The lessons contain some important concepts for students to know, such as the value of work and money management. However, the good parts of "The Yummy Pizza Company" are quickly overshadowed by the fact that 40% of it is about forming Pizza Makers Union Local 18. That's right—the program is focused on teaching kids to unionize.

I don't suppose this creative curriculum has anything do to with current issues, like collective bargaining privileges for public employees. Teachers wouldn't be so blatant as to involve young children in their political issues, would they?

Of course they would—they're leftists! But before students get down to the bare knuckled business of bargaining a contract, there's fun to be had. First, students are told to design a union logo and membership cards. Then students use math to calculate "union dues as a percentage of wages." (Art, math, social studies—this Big Labor lesson plan is thoughtfully designed to satisfy all kinds of curriculum requirements.)

What's next? Contract negotiations, of course! Yes, elementary kids are then taught the finer points of collectively bargaining for a contract, after which members of the Pizza Makers Union may "vote to accept offer, negotiate further, or strike."

The next lesson covers "unions in the real world," where "students will learn about a real union and how it helped its members," as well as "some labor history and a few prominent labor leaders."

Kids are then encouraged to interview their parents about whether or not they belong to a labor union. Additionally, students will "act out the life of a labor leader." One wonders how students will manage to depict the thuggery that union bosses have become famous for, without running afoul of the school's code of conduct.

The end of the curriculum includes a testimonial from San Francisco teacher Bill Morgan, who gives a first-hand account of his experience with these lessons.

> "Like many teachers involved in the labor movement,
> I have tried to bring labor and workplace issues into my
> classroom. The best I could manage was some isolated
> history lessons about this or that strike, or some organizer
> who showed exemplary courage or dedication."

But Morgan felt he needed a stronger lesson to drive his point home. He decided to utilize the "Yummy Pizza" lesson plan. Still, Morgan wanted to ensure that students fully understood the difficulties of union life.

"At this point, I decided, as the Curriculum stipulates, to explore the down side of management—labor relations," Morgan writes. To accomplish this, he decided to cut students' pay in the classroom Yummy Pizza shop.

> "This is where the lesson became reality. A storm of protest arose, and many of the students decided to follow the example of Cesar Chavez (who we were studying) and go on strike. Twenty-one of the twenty-seven students present that day voted to strike, and strike they did. With my few faithful scabs, I tried to make pizza that next day. Strikers kept coming over to them, trying to convince them to walk out. Three did, and I was left with only three helpers. When we went downstairs to the yard to see our pizza cookies, things got uglier. Picketers walked back and forth in front of our stand, strikers came up and sneezed on the cookies, and told the other kids not to buy them and a scuffle broke out over a sign."

Are you freaking kidding me? The teacher stood by as students sneezed on cookies others were buying to eat?

Disgusting as that is, Morgan was satisfied that his students had been successfully indoctrinated.

". . . [W]e were able to confront in an organic, not imposed way, some of the central economic and social issues of our society," Morgan writes. "I would encourage anyone who is interested in labor and workplace issues to use the 'Yummy Pizza' curriculum."

These 20 hours of educational time are little more than a back door way for labor unions and their most strident activists to foist their propaganda onto innocent elementary students. It is critical that parents are aware of this insidious pro-union curriculum which masquerades as a fun pro-business learning plan.

But "The Yummy Pizza Company" isn't the only way progressives are bringing their "how to be a good union member" agenda into the classroom.

In nearby Berkeley, 2nd grade teacher Margot Pepper explained in a 2007 edition of *Race, Poverty & the Environment,* "For over a decade I've been teaching my six-, seven-, and eight-year-old students to strike against me."[16] Like Morgan, Pepper acts like the mean boss and uses contentious role-playing exercises to lead students to specific conclusions about labor unions.

> "... I give workers hints, like reading *Si Se Puede* by Diana Cohn, about the Los Angeles Janitor's strike, or encouraging them to engage in a tug of war with me over a jump rope in which they all have to join together to bring me down. One year, students snuck into the classroom and made picket signs out of construction paper, masking tape, and poles made of linked markers or meter sticks. I've found it's best to demote supervisors to a non-managerial position just as we go to lunch, so they will feel a sense of solidarity with workers, instead of terrorizing them into complacency, as nearly happened this year.

> "Once workers realize I'm powerless before their united action, they immediately overthrow all class rules. They scream until I surrender. After the class quiets down, I quickly explain that some rules exist to benefit the boss, the others, for the good of all. They ratify each rule anew, and have consistently thrown out the new contract as benefiting only their employer."

A few of those kids are bound to take their "lesson" (and the anti-employer attitude they learned) into the workplace after they graduate. They will learn the hard way that shouting down the boss or sneaking into a supply closet to make protest signs won't fly in the real world. When they are fired, they can contact Ms. Pepper and tell her that her strategy sometimes backfires.

But practical considerations like that mean little to socialists. They realize they don't need to win political office to change America. They can do it through education, the arts and the media. Changing culture in general, they know, will be far more damaging to the American experiment and harder to undo than any election. That's clearly their strategy.

CHAPTER 26

Students Learn How to Negotiate a Teachers' Contract

In the late 1990s, the Los Angeles Unified School District partnered with United Teachers Los Angeles—funded by a federal grant—to produce a multi-part curriculum entitled, "Workplace Issues and Collective Bargaining in the Classroom."[17]

Education Action Group obtained it from the California Department of Education.

The purpose of the curriculum is to get students to appreciate the need for collective bargaining, and experience first-hand how it works. During the lessons, which can take up to a week of class time, students pose as either "labor" or "management" and bargain a teachers' contract. They grapple with such issues as health insurance co-pays, raises and hiring procedures. Finally, the union has someone to feel its pain!

The curriculum includes a video which touts the success of the program. It's insightful that the very first speaker on the video is the former president of the teachers union, A.J. Duffy:

> "UTLA plays a unique role in the labor movement in L.A. As the second largest teachers union in the country, with all of our other responsibilities, we are in the position to educate the next generation of civic leaders by reaching out to high school students and having them participate in a unique UTLA program ... The Collective Bargaining Education Project brings the lessons of labor to the classroom by involving students in the same process

UTLA and other unions engage in to gain better wages
and working conditions for teachers and students at L.A.
Unified Schools."[18]

Linda Tubach, one of the curriculum's creators, says, "The students have
a very direct experience with the issues that they're going to face in their
workplaces and their experience is a collective one in small groups, mentored
by coaches who have direct experience in the collective bargaining process."

At the time the video was produced, unionized employees in California
comprised less than 18 percent of the workforce, according to the federal
Bureau of Labor Statistics.[19] In other words, Tubach's lessons may never
apply to 80 percent of these future workers. But, of course, that isn't what
the lessons are about. They're about ginning up awareness and sympathy for
organized labor, so the movement will grow. The lessons are not designed to
prepare students for the world as it is—they prepare kids for the world as
the left *wants* it to be. One in which future workers insist on unionization,
whether it's necessary or not.

The lesson is confrontation in the workplace, whether it's necessary or not.

Alberto Valdivia, then UTLA treasurer, has nothing but praise for the lessons.

"This is really, really wonderful," Valdivia says in the video. "And the
reason that it's wonderful is because it's the students who are making the
decisions . . . Here you have this whole setup that is made for student
enrichment, for student learning, for student knowledge."[20]

Viewers hear from more union officials and allies who are eager to heap praise
upon the curriculum. "I would think that this is one of the most valuable
tools that the L.A. Unified School District has," notes Miguel Contreras,
Executive Secretary-Treasurer of the L.A. County Federation of Labor.

"The vast majority of students will be entering the workforce in the next
few years and it's very important that they understand the role of unions,"
says Kent Wong of the UCLA Center for Labor Research and Education.
"It's very important that they understand the benefits of having a union
contract and the role of collective bargaining in an environment that

provides the only opportunity for workers to collectively negotiate their wages and their benefits."

It appears that the curriculum is having its desired effect on students.

In the video, one student says, "It makes me—when I get my career or my job—it's going to make me want to get into a union, too, so that I'll be protected, too."

Amidst all this pro-union propaganda, parents and taxpayers are left to wonder if any part of LAUSD's curriculum teaches students about how to start a business of their own, or how society and the American economy benefit from the entrepreneurial spirit.

It's safe to assume that the Los Angeles school district cannot be bothered with pro-free market messages which would only distract from the mission of creating the next generation of labor leaders and activists.

In 2000, the school district issued a memo indicating that, "In two years, this [UTLA] program has directly served more than 80 teachers and their students in 39 LAUSD high schools. Almost 5,000 students have directly participated in a collective bargaining simulation."[21]

At long last, school administrators and union leaders are working together. It's too bad their joint venture doesn't involve anything that benefits students.

While it is difficult to nail down just how widespread the curriculum is outside of Los Angeles, the organizers claim they've received requests from school districts across the country to bring it to their communities.

Parents and taxpayers are assured that the curriculum aligns with the District's learning standards, as well as the California History-Social Science Framework. That says something about California learning standards, doesn't it?

The fact that schools from across the country want to use this curriculum says a lot about the state of American public education, too.

CHAPTER 27

Unions Teach Students about . . . Unions

Talk about a captive audience. The California Federation of Teachers has produced a multi-lesson curriculum on labor history to be delivered to children by unionized teachers. Entitled "Golden Lands, Working Hands," the curricula is nothing less than pure Big Labor propaganda.[22]

According to a 1994 edition of the *Labor Center Reporter*, the curriculum takes 6 weeks of class time and will "instruct high school students on the history of the California labor movement." It also states that the curriculum was paid for by unions "interested in seeing labor education taught in our schools."[23]

Included in the "Golden Lands" curriculum is the "Labor History Rap," which goes a little something like this:

> "The rest worked themselves to death back when there was no minimum wage/ The age of railroads meant mass transportation/ But did rich men make the trains of our nation?/ Psych! It was the working people who laid the tracks/ . . . And see who did the work who got the job done/ While lazy lone ranger was out havin' fun . . ."[24]

The rap is presented in the form of a music video. After the minimum wage line, the cartoon character in the video falls into the grave he just dug. Then, a pig rises out of a pile of money bags. You must see the video with your own eyes.

But it doesn't end there. Teachers are provided with a series of questions to ask students. The curriculum thoughtfully provides the correct answers, just in case students don't reach the union-approved conclusions on their own. So much for teaching the art of critical thinking.

The lesson plan reads:

> **"Why do workers need labor unions?**
> *To deal with the power of business owners, working united in an organization that can negotiate collectively and take other collective action to achieve their goals.*

> **"Do unions already have too much power?**
> *Union membership was the highest in the early 1950s, when unions represented about 35% of all workers. Today union membership has declined to about 12% with both private business and public sector employment combined. Just 8% of all private business and industry in the U.S. is unionized."*

Interesting. The writers didn't even answer their own question.

> **"Don't unions force workers into strikes?**
> *. . . Generally, they only strike when the boss is extremely unreasonable—after all, workers give up their paychecks when they go on strike together! . . . Strike violence is rare—and rarely unprovoked. It is also important to realize that workers in this country lack an effective right to strike, because in the U.S., employers can permanently replace striking workers."*

In two other lessons from the "Golden Lands" curriculum, students are taught about Socialist leaders, such as Eugene Debs and his union. They are asked to ponder the following quote:

> "The issue is Socialism versus Capitalism. I am for Socialism because I am for humanity. We have been cursed with the reign of gold long enough. Money constitutes no proper basis of civilization. The time has come to regenerate society, we're on the eve of a universal change."

Students then pretend to be in Debs' Industrial Workers of the World union. The lesson reads:

> ". . . You believe that all wealth is produced by the workers, so all wealth should be controlled by the workers—what do owners produce?

> "Thus, the goal of the IWW is not only for higher wages or shorter hours, but to change the whole society. Workplaces and all of society should be run by the people who produce, the people who do the work . . . The (American Federation of Labor) seems to be afraid of strikes. The IWW isn't. What better learning experience could there be than a confrontation between capitalists and workers? A strike allows the IWW to illustrate to workers that, 'The capitalist class and the working class have nothing in common.'"

But the lessons aren't reserved just for the virtues of Big Labor. Students also are required to write a poem "using the themes" from one written by German Marxist Bertolt Brecht, the namesake of the New York City-based Brecht Forum.[25]

The assignment reads:

> "As a prompt, you might suggest they begin with a question as Brecht does, but with a current event or fact stimulating the thinking process, e.g., the fact that the average yearly compensation for Chief Executive Officers (CEOs) of the 500 largest corporations averages more than 430 times the salary of the average worker employed by them."[26]

Smearing capitalism. Mimicking Marxist poets. Does free-market America stand any chance against the constant assault taking place in our government school classrooms? Do young minds stand any chance of forming independent opinions and conclusions?

In an interview with the *Labor Center Reporter*, Fred Glass of the California Federation of Teachers explains the curriculum's purpose: "It will give [students] the knowledge necessary to be able to say, 'Union Yes!' if they are working in a place where they have that choice."[27]

CHAPTER 28

Hitler 'Admired Ford's Philosophy'!

When unionized teachers tell the history of Ford Motor Company, it's no accident that the United Auto Workers are glorified and Henry Ford is smeared.

The California Federation of Teachers' "Labor in the Schools Committee" produced "AutoWorks," a comic book-style history of the auto industry.[28] But like so much other union-produced curriculum, it doesn't highlight the innovation of an entrepreneur who revolutionized manufacturing, changed America and provided jobs and mobility for millions of people. Instead, it focuses on unionization efforts and the evil entrepreneur's supposed attempts to sabotage them.

In typical leftist fashion, "AutoWorks" takes subtle digs at America. In its ever-so-brief history of the evolution of automobiles, there is an image of some sort of military leader fueling his sedan, with the quotation "Cars affect all kinds of things. Take oil, for instance. The United States has gone to war more than once to make sure there would be lots of oil available—for what? To have gas for cars and trucks . . ."

Henry Ford is shown no mercy. The comic book asserts that, "Not only did Henry Ford think he could control how his workers worked, but how they lived and thought as well!"

In case that wasn't evil enough, consider this doozy: "Henry Ford seemed to be a friend of working people at first, but as he became rich, he had turned into a dictator. In fact, Adolph Hitler studied and admired Ford's philosophy! Henry Ford ruled his factories with an iron hand, and he hated unions."

The inference is clear: Ford's monetary success made him turn so evil that Hitler studied *him*! Who knew they had gas chambers and concentration camps in Detroit, Michigan?

Another bit of union-driven history revisionism suggests that the Great Depression was caused by business owners:

> "Soon, Ford produced more cars than people could buy. Other business owners made the same mistake, and workers were fired. So many people lost jobs that the 1930s were called 'The Great Depression.'"

The "book" argues that as employees saw compensation fall (most likely because there were more workers for fewer jobs) the UAW rose like a phoenix to save all man-, er, human-kind. "AutoWorks" readers are told that the most glorious thing the union did was to refuse to work. When the UAW went on strike, it showed Ford who the real boss was, much as it did during the last few decades of the 20th century, when union-negotiated wages and benefits almost brought about the collapse of the American auto industry. Of course, that's never mentioned in "AutoWorks."

The more the union controls curriculum in America's schools, the more we'll see history revised to suit Big Labor's agenda.

CHAPTER 29

A Fact-Free Approach to Teaching Labor History

The famous songwriter/performer Paul Simon once sang, "*If I think back on all the crap I learned in high school/ It's a wonder I can think at all.*"

Any student who had the misfortune of participating in The Organic Goodie Simulation can empathize with Simon's views on public education.

I found the "Organic Goodie Simulation" lesson in "The Power in Our Hands: A Curriculum on the History of Work and Workers in the United States."[29] This simulation/lesson plan purports to teach students about the history of organized labor, although it's light on historical fact and heavy on the "organic" material, if you catch my drift.

Observers of the American political scene understand that fanning the flames of envy is the main way the left advances its political agenda (i.e. fighting budget cuts that hurt "working families" and pressing for tax increases that require the "wealthiest one percent to pay their fair share").

Without envy, there would be no labor unions. So I guess it's only natural that the goal of a popular lesson plan about organized labor is to generate discord among the students. These kids must see themselves as the future "workers of the world" and know how to properly organize, right? The tricky part is getting kids to turn off their cell phones, iPods and Xboxes long enough to understand just how oppressed they really are.

The Organic Goodie Simulation accomplishes this by presenting class warfare in a "fun" manner.

Teachers are instructed to:

> "Close the door and the blinds in the classroom. Tell
> students to imagine that we are going to live in this
> classroom for the rest of our lives (many groans). Explain
> that there is no soil for farming but we are in luck because
> we have a machine that produces food—organic goodies.
> Then correct yourself and point out that actually you own
> the machine."

Savvy readers can see where this is going, but in case you went to the same
school as Paul Simon, here's the upshot of the lesson:

The owner of the "goodie" machine needs workers to help run it. Half the
students are hired, while the other half remains unemployed. The workers
are paid just enough to survive, while the unemployed are given just enough
in welfare benefits to slowly starve to death.

Here's where the fun begins. The teacher/owner wants to improve his profit
margin, so he cuts wages, pitting the workers against the unemployed. The
owner then hires a student to be his foreman and a few students to be his
police force.

Will the students see that their only hope is to organize into a labor union?
Or will the workers revolt and claim the goodie machine for the people? Or
will hopelessness and lack of cooperation doom a large number of them to
"starve" to death?

Teachers are instructed, "The game ends when students have had ample
opportunity to organize successfully or otherwise. Participants may be
totally demoralized—beaten down—or they may have taken over the
machine."

Day Two of the simulation is set aside for student reflection. A series of
probing questions is provided. Here are a few highlights:

> "As the owner, what kind of attitudes would I want you to
> have about your ability to work together as a unified group?"

"Why do people have a hard time working together for common goals? Is it because of human nature? Is it because of what people are taught or the pressures they're under?"

I'll admit that "The Organic Goodie Simulation" might be kind of fun (except for all the collateral damage, of course). The problem with this lesson is its near-total detachment from actual U.S. history.

Go back to the beginning when the students were told "we are going to have to live in this classroom for the rest of our lives" and "there is no soil for farming."

Think about how those statements completely contradict why and how this country was formed.

America was settled by immigrants who left their motherlands in search of better lives for themselves and their families. All throughout our history, people have left economically-intolerable and politically-oppressive situations to seek out better opportunities in America.

When the cotton fields proved insufficient, a large number of Americans went to work in the factories of the North. The more adventurous souls headed for the open spaces of the West.

Today, people use higher education as a means of seeking out a better life, migrating from small towns to large universities.

Think of it this way: It's not inconceivable that a poor farmer or factory worker in the early 1900s might have had grandchildren who went on to graduate from college in the '50s and '60s. Ours is a society of opportunity and upward mobility.

But that doesn't fit the agenda of the labor unions, or this "history" lesson which trains students to see the world in terms of have and have-nots, oppressors and victims. That's the real lesson being pushed by the "Organic Goodie Simulation" which, by the way, seems to have achieved a place of honor in high school social studies classrooms throughout the nation.

In 2002, teacher Greg Queen praised the Simulation in his paper titled "Using Marx as the Fountainhead in Secondary Social Studies Curriculum Organization: A Rationale."

Queen writes:

> "One particular resource that I think has been valuable . . . is a curriculum on the history of work and workers in the United States titled *Power in our Hands*. The curriculum materials encourage those who experience the lessons to reflect 'on our power, our ability to make and remake society—to see everything about our lives as changeable.' . . . The lesson that has the most impact is the *Organic Goodie Simulation* . . . A student who experienced the Organic Goodie simulation said he learned a lot about being controlled or having control over people . . ."[30]

[Queen is now a teacher in Warren, Michigan, where he told the World Socialist Web Site that a "united strike action by teachers" should be the response to education reforms that were passed by the state lawmakers in early 2011.[31]]

Sounds like the simulation is meeting its unstated goal of inspiring a new generation of labor organizers.

Like most organic products, the Organic Goodie Simulation makes heavy use of manure to create its final product.

'AMERICA' IS SOOO LAST CENTURY

The children who know how to think for themselves
spoil the harmony of the collective society which is
coming, where everyone would be interdependent.
—John Dewey, American educator

CHAPTER 30

Creating 'Global Citizens'

There is a disturbing trend in America's public schools which is emphasizing "global citizenship" at the expense of American Exceptionalism. The "Blame America" crowd wants students to believe America uses too much energy, produces too much waste, hordes too many resources and takes food out of the mouths of people in the third world. They call for a redistribution of world resources, which, by their math, would result in a drastic change in the lifestyle and standard of living for Americans.

While they don't like to discuss their redistribution plans publicly, they're nonetheless very serious about planting these ideas in kids' heads.

Imagine wiping the state lines off the United States map. Fiscally responsible states like Wisconsin would now have to bear the burden of blundering states like California. Resource-rich regions like the Great Lakes would have to pump fresh water to arid regions like the desert Southwest. There would be fundamental changes that would create great upheaval for many Americans.

The Blame America crowd wants to do the same thing on the global level. America would have no borders. Our financial and natural resources would be redistributed around the world. In order to become global citizens, Americans would have to adjust to a much lower standard of living. For example, being a good global citizen would mean getting serious about global warming. That would likely require that Americans pay a lot more for a gallon of gas, which would end up reducing a family's mobility and alter its day-to-day lifestyle decisions.

Being a good global citizen probably doesn't sound too appealing to you, but it's high on the progressives' to-do list. The left knows that American adults will resist their efforts. That's why they are training our children not only to accept global citizenship as normal and inevitable, but to actively work for it.

The American Forum for Global Education wondered in a 2001-2002 newsletter:

> "Can there ever be a 'citizen of the world?' That is, a citizen who does not owe allegiance to one single community, state, or nation, but rather owes allegiance to the entire human race—without boundaries, without regard to race, ethnicity, social/economic condition, or place of birth? . . . The two words [world and citizenship] together seem paradoxical. 'You can educate either the citizen or the man,' wrote Thoreau. Yet in their union lies the potential success of the human species; in their non-union lies the demise of a fatally-flawed creature that could not overcome its self-imposed global anarchy."[1]

Wow! To tackle this life-threatening issue—and avert apparent anarchy—the Forum provides a "Curriculum for Global Citizenship" lesson which was developed by Oxfam GB, a British charity dedicated to fighting global poverty.

The lesson explains, "Educating young people to become Global Citizens will ensure that they are able to work for a more secure and sustainable future."[2]

This was produced a decade ago. Since then, anti-American globalists have found numerous other ways to subvert the greatest country in the history of the world, as upcoming chapters will explain.

CHAPTER 31

Good Global Citizens Are Made, Not Born

The U.S. in its current form is a detriment to the "global community," according to the progressive school of thought. And if the pantywaists at the United Nations had their way, America would be reduced to the status of Papua New Guinea or some other country that exerts little influence on the world's affairs. That's the logical conclusion of a 7-part series of lessons produced by the U.N. Department of Public Information.

In the U.N.'s "Equal Dignity and Worth" lesson, students learn:

> "In this changing era people are busy trying to find their own identities as individuals, as ethnic or cultural groups and as nations. Unfortunately many think that 'pride' or 'self-esteem' also means feeling superior to someone else—that those not as 'good' or 'rich' or 'intelligent' should be excluded."[3]

I hope that isn't referring to the U.S. The last time I checked, America "excludes" very few other nations, particularly when it comes to foreign aid. We are the biggest benefactor on Earth, and give generously to less fortunate nations and populations.

The lesson also echoes the U.N.'s call for "a fairer share in the responsibilities and opportunities and benefits related to international economic activity" and seeks to find "the means for constructing a more sensible and just world community."

I think they're saying Americans should be forced to share the wealth that we've worked so hard over the generations to earn. The lesson goes on to explain how that will make us feel better about ourselves: "You may feel that these new ideas and experiences have released you from fears and prejudices—that your spirit is free to soar—that you can grow and fulfill your special capabilities." Where is my peace pipe? I must have a toke now!

Another U.N. lesson, "More and Less," is further proof that in the end, America comes out on the short end of the U.N.'s stick. "Consumerism is a theme that preoccupies many young people," the lesson reads. "There is enough material substance and technical knowledge in the world to feed, clothe, shelter, educate and transport many more people than this planet now holds, but we have population and development 'problems' because of our refusal to allocate resources equitably."[4]

Again, the American government gives away a lot, and much of it is wasted by foreign governments and never repaid. The folks at the U.N. know that and don't seem to care. Should we penalize ourselves even further for having a successful economy and enjoying the fruits of our labor?

In a role play that accompanies the "Serving the World" lesson[5], students pose as U.N. filmmakers bantering ideas "appropriate to the U.N. in the twenty-first century." One idea? Have them discuss the so-called "Law of the Sea."

Here's an excerpt from the role play:

> "[**Director of Film Division Shib**] **Rawat:** Let's move on to the second idea. Irina . . .

> "[**Film director Irina**] **Ivanov:** Recently in the General Assembly the Secretary-General called the U.N. Convention on the Law of the Sea a 'Milestone in the building of a true community of nations.' If we did a film telling the remarkable story of the Law of the Sea, young people might realize how far the U.N. has come. For 50 years the U.N. has been moving away from a world of competing member states and towards—well, here we have something totally new—a legal order of the oceans.

"[**Film writer Han**] **Ling:** There's even more than that. The Convention declares the seabed and its resources as the common heritage of humankind. It could unite the world community in its quest to preserve our planet for generations to come."[6]

Students mindlessly role play the U.N.'s strategy to undermine America.

This is a real threat to America's sovereignty and students are learning it in government schools. In the "We Organize" lesson, the U.N. makes clear its intent with the series:

"Later in their schooling pupils will learn to discover the patterns of world movements and the individual's own place in them. The U.N. is a good tool for these discoveries. The United Nations is a fact—a major step in human development. To omit it from the curricula or to focus on only one aspect or ignore its accomplishments distorts history.

"Finding order is especially important now. Submerged in new information, people are shaken by seemingly chaotic events or meaningless violence. Pupils are reassured knowing that there is a world organization keeping watch over the changes.

"To fully understand the U.N., however, pupils must know that the future is in doubt. The United Nations is an experiment. It requires that everyone join in an active search for better ways to live. In the U.N. charter, we have agreed on standards, an organization, and what we want to do, but will we do it?"[7]

Well, will we America? Will you nod in approval when your 7th grader comes home spouting this propaganda? In their quest to create good global citizens, the progressives are hoping that you will.

CHAPTER 32

World Poverty: Made in the USA?

Spend a little time among progressives and you're likely to hear this oft-repeated statistic: "Americans are only 5 percent of the world's population, but they consume 25 percent of the world's energy."

To leftists, this is a damning indictment of American greed and the inequality created by free markets and capitalism. Small wonder the statistic gets repeated ad nauseum on college campuses and throughout the blogosphere.

With so much of the world's population mired in misery, one would think the international community would study how the principles of individual liberty, free markets and the rule of law helped the United States became prosperous and powerful. Instead of looking for a handout, they could learn a lesson about self-reliance.

But those principles are anathema to the busybody Marxists who seek to control nearly every facet of life on Earth. So instead of promoting American values, the left sneers at them. Worse, the progressives use the public school system to teach our children that the American way is to blame for much of the world's suffering.

This anti-American mindset is the basis of the widely distributed lesson plan "World Poverty and World Resources." The lesson plan was written by Susan Hersh and Bob Peterson, and is disseminated by the leftists at "Rethinking Schools."[8] Peterson is currently the president of the Milwaukee teachers' union.

The lesson begins with teachers familiarizing their students with the following terms: *resources, Gross National Product, wealth, distribution, income, power* and *colonialism*. Notice that the terms *freedom, free markets, private property rights,* and *rule of law* are not mentioned, which is a dead giveaway of where this lesson is headed.

After the vocabulary warm-up, students are given 25 poker chips to represent the world's population of 6.5 billion people. Simple division reveals that each chip represents about 260 million people. (This represents the most academically-rigorous portion of the lesson plan.) Using a world map and census figures, students then place chips on each continent to represent how the world's population is distributed.

Next, students are given 25 poker chips of a different color to represent the world's wealth (or Gross National Product). The "wealth" chips are distributed among the continents according to GNP numbers. To underscore the lesson's anti-American message, students are told that Mexico will be considered part of Latin America, leaving the United States and Canada to represent North America.

Once that is done, students are asked to "reflect on the sizes of the two different sets of chip stacks, representing population and resources." The obvious implication is that the U.S. and other Western countries have an unfair share of the world's resources.

The lesson has a few more convoluted steps involving role play and chocolate chip cookies (whoever said America bashing couldn't be fun—and delicious?), but those uneven stacks of chips represent the heart of the lesson.

To drive the point home, teachers are told to conclude the lesson with a class discussion. The authors even provide a list of questions "worth posing if students don't ask them themselves," such as:

+ How did the distribution of wealth get so unequal?
+ Who do you think decides how wealth is distributed?
+ Should wealth be distributed equally?
+ What can be done about the unequal way wealth is distributed?

Teachers are advised to assign students follow-up research on "the role colonialism played in the wealth disparity" and "how current policies of U.S. corporations and the U.S. government affect people in poorer nations."

Students are left to conclude that the United States is wealthy either through dumb luck or by outright theft. No mention is made of how an individual's right to private property and the rule of law create conditions that allow economies to thrive. Nothing is mentioned about the American work ethic or American ingenuity which has raised the standard of living for people across the planet. Even Communist China acknowledges the power of free markets (to a certain degree), and has seen its economy grow leaps and bounds as a result.

But developing an understanding and appreciation of free markets and capitalism is not the lesson's goal. It's not even designed to develop critical thought. Instead, the lesson seeks to create feelings of guilt and shame within students, and sell them on the need for wealth redistribution.

The lesson does not tell students that poverty and hunger have posed major problems all throughout human history. What is needed is a lesson plan that explains to children that American and Western capitalism has freed untold billions of people from the worries of hunger and abject poverty.

Here's one example: Innovations in farming (spurred on by the capitalistic desire to make a profit) have allowed America to become the world's leading exporter of corn and a major exporter of grain.[9] Capitalism is literally helping to feed the world.

But that doesn't fit the social justice agenda, either. So expect to see more lesson plans like this one which blame American-style capitalism (which has been around for just over 200 years) for the world's problems of poverty, hunger and misery, all of which have been around since the beginning of human history.

CHAPTER 33

'No Human is Illegal'

In the progressives' zeal for One World—not to mention their belief in a disputed border between the United States and Mexico—activists have turned to the classroom to indoctrinate students about the travesty of illegal immigration.

But you would be wrong if you assumed that these teachers believe American law should be enforced. No, they believe American law is the problem and should simply be wiped off the books. They believe anyone should be able to come across the border at will and reap the benefits of America: free public education, free Medicaid and other components of our wide and generous social safety net.

To advance this view point, the New York Collective of Radical Educators (NYCoRE) has created a lesson plan titled, "No Human is Illegal." NYCoRE describes itself as, "a group of public school educators committed to fighting for social justice in our school system and society at large, by organizing and mobilizing teachers, developing curriculum, and working with community, parent, and student organizations."

In response to a federal immigration reform bill in 2006, NYCoRE recommended three levels of action for teachers and students:

1. Participate with NYCoRE in the May 1ˢᵗ Great American Boycott.
2. Encourage and protect students who participate in the May 1ˢᵗ action.
3. Connect your activism to your academics.[10]

May 1st, of course, is a day when socialists, communists, anarchists and unionists protest—sometimes violently—around the world against "the man." So on May 1st and the days leading up to it, NYCoRE instructs teachers to "bring these concepts from the streets into the classroom and then back onto the streets—united as teacher and student activists in the struggle for human rights for all humans—because, no human is illegal!"

In terms of bringing it into the classroom, the lesson suggests students role-play different identities (documented, undocumented, and newer immigrants) and how legislation would affect them, reviewing the pros and cons of protests, boycotts, walkouts—including boycotting school!—as well as reviewing articles from the World Socialist Web Site.

The lesson plan also encourages students to visit the websites of organizations such as the Minute Man Project, but warns, "These sites are extremely racist and should be well framed before visited by students."

As students and teachers review the activism of pro-amnesty activists around the country, one Arizona teacher has been putting it to action.

Interviewed in the NYCoRE Social Justice Plan Book (see Chapter 11), Tucson 11th and 12th grade literature teacher and "teacher activist" Curtis Acosta explained his classes "explore feminist literature, African American lit, LGBT writing, critically conscious hip-hop and much more while continuing to explore the stories and work of Chicanos/Latinos."[11]

A *New York Times* reporter visited Acosta's classroom and found that, "The class began with a Mayan-inspired chant and a vigorous round of coordinated hand clapping."[12]

The Arizona legislature moved to end controversial racially-based curriculum, such as Acosta's. True to his activist roots, he didn't take it lightly. He sued the state. "In addition to the lawsuit, our students, teachers, parents and community members have been active through civil disobedience and peaceful protests that have varied in scope. We have performed a ceremonial run from Tucson to Phoenix during the searing heat of the Arizona summer, a human chain vigil, teatro, marches and many rallies at school board meetings," Acosta said in the plan book.[13]

The "rallies," as he describes them, have been less than civil. In addition to calling for Tuscon Superintendent John Pedicone to resign, students stormed an April 2011 school board meeting, commandeering board members' seats, pounding on the table, chanting *"fight back"* with a wild—if not demonic—look in their eyes. The meeting was canceled.

The *Times* article noted that Acosta has brought his fight with politicians into the classroom as well:

> "'It's propagandizing and brainwashing that's going on there,' Tom Horne, Arizona's newly elected attorney general, said this week as he officially declared the program in violation of a state law that went into effect on Jan. 1."

The article seemed to verify Horne's position:

> "Although Shakespeare's 'Tempest' was supposed to be the topic at hand, Mr. Acosta spent most of a recent class discussing the political storm in which he, his students and the entire district have become enmeshed. Mr. Horne's name came up more than once, and not in a flattering light."[14]

Fox 10 in Phoenix reported that students could take this course *in place* of an American history class.[15] With all of this handclapping, hip-hop music and LGBT literature, who has time to learn about those rich, white fuddy-duddies who wrote the U.S. Constitution?

Acosta was quoted as saying in the "Social Justice Plan Book":

> "... What is happening to us in Arizona is part of a larger context and assault upon civil and human rights for Chicanos and Latinos in the United States. Political rherotic in our state is toxic, as our own Sheriff Clarence Dupnik said after the horrific shootings in our city on January 8th of 2011; and this is leading to more dehumanizing actions and policies."

Political rhetoric is toxic, indeed. And it's filling the minds of countless students to fulfill the progressives' political agenda.

CHAPTER 34

How Mickey Mouse Terrorized Haiti

On January 12, 2010, a 7.0 earthquake mercilessly shook the country of Haiti, causing death and destruction of Biblical proportions. By the time the last aftershock was registered, approximately 85,000 Haitians were dead, and hundreds of thousands more were injured or left homeless.[16]

Some observed that the 1989 San Francisco earthquake also reached 7.0 on the Richter scale, but that quake left 63 people dead and left about 12,000 homeless.[17] The difference between the two was that California's buildings are designed to withstand powerful earthquakes, and Haiti's are not.

That realization brought renewed attention to the poverty of the Haitian people. Onlookers began to question why the tiny Caribbean country was so ill-prepared for an earthquake . . . and so hopelessly poor, in general.

One observer suggested a possible reason:

> "In Haiti's 200-year quest for freedom, one of the most crucial components of freedom, which leads to prosperity, has never been effectively implemented or even seriously tried (much less respected). The Haitian system of establishing property rights is so convoluted, complicated and corrupt that to the average citizen of Haiti owning any property will always remain just a dream. The connection between poverty and the lack of property rights is often overlooked."[18]

George Mason University economist Walter Williams noted that the rule of law is virtually nonexistent in Haiti:

> "Crime and lawlessness are rampant in Haiti. The U.S. Department of State Web site . . . long before the earthquake warned, *There are no 'safe' areas in Haiti . . . Kidnapping, death threats, murders, drug-related shootouts, armed robberies, home break-ins and car-jacking are common in Haiti . . .* Crime anywhere is a prohibitive tax on economic development, and the poorest people are its primary victims."[19]

A thoughtful social studies teacher could contrast the Haiti and San Francisco earthquakes as a way of teaching students about property rights and the rule of law (versus the rule of the mob or dictator). Students could learn that without the rule of law, individuals could not enjoy their natural, God-given rights of life, liberty and the pursuit of happiness, as set forth in our Declaration of Independence.

Of course, discussing Haiti in those terms would lead to an affirmation of the American way of life—individual liberties and economic freedoms—and that clearly doesn't meet the goals of the Blame America First/Social Justice crowd that currently controls public education.

As such, when Haiti gets discussed in our public schools, it's likely the Haitian people are depicted as victims of greedy capitalists who are trapped in poverty because U.S. corporations have turned Haiti into America's sweatshop, making the products that fill our superstores.

That's the premise behind "Mickey Mouse Goes to Haiti," a 1996 documentary that was produced by the National Labor Committee and has infiltrated elementary social studies classrooms all across the country.

The documentary opens with an unidentified man speaking outside of a Disney store:

> "The profits that are made by the fashion industry and these conglomerates are astronomical. And not to be concerned for the people's lives is a totally disastrous attitude—especially from a company like Walt Disney that makes their living . . . on children."[20]

After asserting that the Disney corporation pays workers seven cents to produce a shirt that will sell for $12, the filmmakers document the squalid living conditions of the Haitian workers.

The film spends most of its 28-minute run time claiming that U.S. companies are attracted to poverty-stricken Haiti to exploit its people. The film also suggests that there are so many Haitian workers that companies can play the unemployed against the workers to keep wages low. The message is very clear for viewers (specifically students): Profit-seeking corporations are the cause of Haiti's suffering.

At one point in the film, a Haitian worker looks into the camera and says, "I'd like to send a message to the American people. If they send these clothes to be made in Haiti, if the Americans can't give a living wage to us, to the Haitian workers, they shouldn't wear the clothes we have made for them in Haiti. That would be better for us."

Suppose you're a fifth-grade student who is watching "Mickey Mouse Goes to Haiti" as part of a multi-week unit plan titled, "Work, Workers & the U.S. Labor Movement."[21] What conclusions are you going to draw about corporations? About free markets and capitalism? About the American way of life in general?

Is there another side to this story? Would someone please share it with the kids?

A blog post written by a student who claims to have watched the documentary in school provides some answers:

> "There is a documentary . . . I saw last week during my video class. It's called 'Mickey Mouse Goes to Haiti.' In the states, how much can you purchase a Walt Disney t-shirt (for)? $12?

> "This corporation (including others) has factories in 3rd world countries such as Haiti and they pay workers about $0.28 an hour. By the end of the day, they make about $2.88 and about $14.00 at the end of the week.

> "These people work full-time, 7 days a week and they still don't have enough to feed the whole family, never mind medication or saving up for a more promising future . . .

> "People die in third world countries at a rate of about 1 person every 6 seconds, so the next time you go to the Walt Disney store, Disney World or the next hot feature presentation, don't just admire the crews sitting in the office doing something you might want to do for a living, but also the millions who sewed your Lion King t-shirt you just used as a floor towel."[22] (grammar and spelling were corrected for clarity)

The student's anger toward free markets, capitalism and corporations is palpable, which is surely the reaction activist-minded teachers are going for when they show the video.

The intent here is not to excuse corporations that take unfair advantage of employees in third world countries. The American consumer is right to hold such companies accountable for exploitative business practices, and the Haitian government responsible for not establishing and enforcing some fundamental work standards.

However, social justice teachers must also be held accountable for twisting facts and misrepresenting situations to their students. To claim that Haiti is in dire straits because Americans practice capitalism is absurd. If anything, Haitians are suffering because capitalism (which requires property rights) does not exist in their country. Haiti is a land where lawlessness reigns. If the average Haitian tries to get ahead by starting a small business, what chance does he or she have in staving off the band of thieves that will descend upon their store or factory? And whatever the bandits don't steal, the corrupt government will take. Sadly, many Haitians have decided that the sweat shops are their best chance for survival. That makes the sweat shops only a symptom of Haiti's problems, not the cause of them.

My research indicates that "Mickey Mouse Goes to Haiti" is primarily used in fifth grade social studies classes—well before students have a clear understanding of our founding principles. Turning students against a system about which they know almost nothing is more than propaganda; it is educational malpractice.

The history of capitalism is one of freeing individuals to pursue their goals and dreams. The pursuit of profit has led to innumerable inventions and innovations that have improved the quality of life for all humanity. Remember, it was the free market system which allowed for the creation of the life-saving medicines and medical treatments that were delivered to the Haitian people after the 2010 earthquake.

Like all propaganda, "Mickey Mouse Goes to Haiti" distorts reality by telling a skewed and incomplete story. But what makes it truly dangerous is that it might be playing in a classroom near you.

CHAPTER 35

U.N.'s 'Law of the Sea' Trumps National Sovereignty?

Globalists bent on marginalizing America and our prowess have devised a way to create One World: the sea rules. As I touched on in the previous United Nations section, if international laws can govern the seas, then we can inch closer to one world government. This is not conspiracy paranoia—this is fact.

A lesson plan entitled "The Sensible Use of the Shared Seas," states that its purpose is to "lead students to realize the difficulties of reconciling national interests and global environmental concerns while engaging in an interactive activity which tests both their oral and written skills."[23]

But here's the spoiler: "national interests" don't trump "global environmental concerns."

Over four class periods, students engage in a simulation in which they review a map, read about a particular hypothetical country's claims of domain over its environment, the impact on neighboring nations and what the ramifications should be. Some questions include:

- Should there be a national economic zone beyond the territorial limit? If so, how far?
- Do nations have the right to pollute the oceans, whether off their own shores or on the high seas? If not, what should be done about it?
- Should the ocean be considered the common heritage of the people of the world? If so, should an international organization be formed to regulate the mining of the seas

and use a percentage of the profits to foster the development of poorer nations?

It's questions like the last one which identify the lesson's real agenda: a redistribution of wealth by way of a higher authority—an "international organization." It's not just about protecting the oceans, it's about seizing resources from prospering countries and giving them to countries that are not prospering.

Furthermore, students are asked to answer the above questions only after they are given a set of statements, which include the following:

+ Many of the nations of the world believe the oceans are the common heritage of mankind.
+ Most of the poorest countries want an international agency to mine the mineral resources of the seabed and share the profits among nations.[24]

As a middle or high school student, what do you think your answer would be?

This is just a sampling of numerous lesson plans that are bent on turning American students into global citizens. Progressives—employed by government schools and paid with our hard-earned tax dollars—are marginalizing American Exceptionalism at a time when the world needs it most.

TAKING A STAND

In a world where the very idea of "public" is being threatened, for educators to feign neutrality is irresponsible . . . The teacher who takes pride in never revealing his or her "opinions" to students models for them moral apathy.

—Milwaukee teachers union President Bob Peterson and Oregon teacher Bill Bigelow

CHAPTER 36

Below-Average Purveyors of Classroom Marxism

An argument could be made, I suppose, that if American students were outperforming their global peers, they could justifiably spend classroom time on non-essential issues. But we've become the snoozing hare while our competitors have become the determined tortoise. We're either oblivious to that fact or, worse, we're ignoring it.

Several recent reports from the prestigious consulting group McKinsey & Company should serve as an urgent wake-up call for Americans.

An April 2009 McKinsey & Company study found that American students are 25th in mathematics scores and 24th in science scores globally, and we're being outpaced by countries like Iceland and Hungary. The same study found the United States spends the most to achieve such mediocre results.[1]

The study also analyzed national testing data (National Assessment of Educational Progress) and found "48 percent of blacks and 43 percent of Latinos are [academically] 'below basic,' while only 17 percent of whites are, and this gap exists in every state. A more pronounced racial achievement gap exists in most large urban school districts."[2]

"These educational gaps impose on the United States the economic equivalent of a permanent national recession," the report found.

Is it a coincidence that many of the radical lesson plans outlined in this book are generated or found in many urban districts? Is it possible these activist teachers could be largely to blame for such poor minority student performance? Should they be spending a lot more time covering the fundamentals and far less creating young activists?

A 2010 McKinsey report, entitled "Closing the Talent Gap: Attracting and retaining top-third graduates to careers in teaching," gave equally jaw-dropping information about the teaching profession.

The report states:

> "The U.S. . . . recruits most teachers from the bottom two-thirds of college classes, and, for many schools in poor neighborhoods, from the bottom third . . . The late Sandra Feldman, president of the American Federation of Teachers from 1997 to 2004 . . . was open about the problem in an interview in 2003. 'You have in the schools right now, among the teachers who are going to be retiring, *very* smart people,' she said. 'We're not getting in now the same kinds of people. It's disastrous. We've been saying for years now that we're attracting from the bottom third.'"[3]

A blogger who goes by the name "A Conservative Teacher," reported on a *WorldNetDaily* article, which read:

> "In 2001, the National Center for Education Statistics reported the average SAT score for intended education majors to be 481 math and 483 verbal. Only those interested in vocational school, home economics and public affairs scored lower.

> "But while the SAT is considered to be a generally reliable intelligence test, the 2001 SAT is not the same SAT that many of us took prior to attending university. Those 2001 scores on the 1996 SAT, which was replaced this year by the New SAT 2005, are equivalent to pre-1996 SAT scores of 451 math and 403 verbal. In case any education majors are reading this, 451 plus 403 equals a cumulative score of 854.

"Examining an SAT-to-IQ conversion chart calculated from Mensa entrance criteria, a combined 854 indicates that the average IQ of those pursuing an education major is 91, nine points lower than the average IQ of 100. In other words, those who can't read teach whole language."[4]

So some teachers that are bitter and seeking to get back at the world could be bringing these anti-American concepts into the classroom. This by no means is a majority of teachers. In fact, it is likely a very small number. But even a small number, dangerously clustered in underperforming urban schools, is too many because they're eating up precious class time with propaganda that shouldn't be fed into children's sponge-like minds. The most vulnerable kids can't afford to be distracted by a teacher's personal political agenda.

Lisa Graham Keegan was Arizona state superintendent for public instruction in the 1990s. She was also on President George W. Bush's short list to be his first secretary of education. She told me this when I asked her about colleges of education:

> "Unfortunately for those seeking how to present challenging and disciplined instruction, potential young teachers in colleges of education are more likely to be taught a professor's personal doctrine than high quality techniques of instruction.

> "The poster boy for education professors whose beliefs and writings denounce actual instruction and promote personal political philosophies is Bill Ayers. Ayers has never modified his political views, as he had barely moved back 'above ground' when he discovered that teaching could serve as the new canvas on which to display his theories of communal progress. Ayers himself can tell you his views in one of any number of books … many of which are required reading in our nation's colleges of education.

> "Those of us who work daily in education are too familiar with the philosophy Ayers espouses, as it has found a

warm and welcoming home in the very institutions that
are meant to prepare young people to teach children. The
Ayers school is marked by a nearly cultish adherence to
rejecting what he terms the 'capitalist hegemony.'"

This is scary stuff. Is this why we see repeated resistance to such simple
concepts like testing students to measure their academic growth? And
further, why we see scandals like the one in Atlanta, where many teachers
allegedly changed the answers on students' standardized tests?[5]

The social justice movement wants public education to be far more
nebulous than it is today. Activists want classrooms to be their domain, free
of oversight from administrators, parents and taxpayers.

Keegan continues:

"Ayers' call is for teachers to recognize that education
must be a mutual discovery, a way of informing students
that they are incomplete, and that they should seek to be
more human. Any direct instructional methods . . . as in
suggesting to students that certain letters always make
certain sounds, or that the Pythagorean Theorem always
works . . . are seen as attempts to 'colonize' and dehumanize
students. The theory is that if I, as a teacher, tell you what
is true, then you are not free to discover that for yourself.

"This has had not only sobering but poisonous
consequences in American classrooms. It has given rise
to false teaching theories such as 'whole language,' which
posits that students learn to read as they learn to talk . . .
just by being in the presence of literature. No direct,
oppressive instruction required. This calamity gave rise to
unprecedented percentages of illiterate American children
and now adults.

"The view is seen every day in the call to avoid 'teaching
to the test' or 'bubbling in' answers on a test sheet, as

the philosophy of oppression requires you to believe that adhering to a strict set of standards does two nasty things:

1. It requires you to acquiesce to the oppressors, and
2. It negates your ability to show off any other talents you have that may not be a part of the test.

"In short, for the Ayers crowd, standards and testing are oppressive features of a capitalist regime. True learning requires neither, in Ayers' view.

"Meanwhile, back in the real world, the only successful schools we know of rely on a constant feedback loop of instruction followed by gauges of progress against clear standards."

Aside from this disturbing assessment, the kernel of good news is that these indoctrination curriculum problems and nutty philosophies are not necessarily universal. These lesson plans and textbooks are not in every school in America. But the fact that they are being used at all—and the teachers do little to hide their agenda—gives no comfort.

The lessons discussed are planting the seeds of socialism and a general leftward shift in America. Those that develop them and those that bring them into their classrooms know precisely what they're doing.

You need to know who some of them are.

"Rethinking" Education

A series of curriculum books have been published by "Rethinking Schools," a non-profit outfit based in Milwaukee, Wisconsin. It's a collection of social justice teachers whose mission is "firmly committed to equity and to the vision that public education is central to the creation of a humane, caring, multiracial democracy," according to its website.

"Rethinking Schools began as a local effort to address problems such as basal readers, standardized testing, and textbook-dominated curriculum. Since its founding, it has grown into a nationally prominent publisher of educational materials, with subscribers in all 50 states, all 10 Canadian provinces, and many other countries."[6]

In one of several curriculum books geared toward "rethinking" what and how students are taught, the editors of one, "Rethinking Globalization," attempt to answer the question, "Is this book biased?"

"Every curriculum begins from certain convictions about the world, even if they may not be conscious. Neutrality is neither possible nor desirable ... In a world where the very idea of 'public' is being threatened, for **educators to feign neutrality is irresponsible** ...

The teacher who takes pride in never revealing his or her 'opinions' to students models for them moral apathy ... We see a distinct difference between a biased curriculum and a partisan one. Teaching is biased when it ignores multiple perspectives and does not allow interrogation of its own assumptions and propositions. Partisan teaching, on the other hand, invites diversity of opinion but does not lose sight of **the aim of the curriculum: to alert students to global injustice, to seek explanations, and to encourage activism.**"[7] (emphasis added)

This is little more than a rationalization of what is occurring. When you have a Greenpeace activist teacher (see chapter 17), realizing she came on too strong, then easing off to meticulously lay the groundwork for students to come to a particular conclusion on man-made global warming, no one honestly believes her method is unbiased.

The lessons reviewed in this book are the products of activist organizations and teachers acting out of a sense that free markets are to blame for poverty, and that America has too much power and global influence.

American Educational Research Association

This is a 25,000-member organization that claims the mantle of being a "professional organization representing educational researchers."[8]

AERA holds annual conferences where members present papers and academics opine about curriculum and educational methods. In 2004, it passed a "Social Justice Mission Statement," in which it, among other things, "commits itself":

- To promote social justice principles and policies in the conduct of education research; that is, in funding of research and training;
- To disseminate and promote the use of research knowledge and stimulate interest in research on social justice issues related to education.[9]

This may seem like just another gin-and-tonic club for pointy-headed professors, but it's much worse than that. The former domestic terrorist Bill Ayers—yes, *that* Bill Ayers, the same Bill Ayers that Keegan referenced—was the association's recent vice president for "curriculum studies." Additionally, AERA awarded Ayers with its "Social Justice in Education" Award.[10]

When Ayers' radicalism became a topic of the 2008 presidential campaign, his fellow academics rallied around him. Fellow vice president and chair of AERA Special Interest Group on Creation and Utilization of Curriculum Knowledge William H. Schubert, defended Ayers, saying:

> "The fact that Dr. Ayers was elected this year as the vice president of AERA's Division B is a testimony of such a stature and high esteem he holds in the field of education locally, regionally, nationally, and internationally.

> "Bill has written extensively about social justice, democracy, school contexts, and ethics regarding students, families, and educators . . . In many of his scholarly writings, Dr. Ayers has called attention to the role of teachers to

demonstrate greater social responsibility in meeting the needs of children.

"So, when he has been heard to say, 'We didn't do enough,' it is emblematic of his philosophy that all of us, including himself, can do more to work for liberty and justice for all—a value that is deeply human and part of the best of the American creed."[11]

The last quote, of course, is in reference to a *New York Times* article Ayers was quoted in where he said, "I don't regret setting bombs. I feel we didn't do enough." The article was published September 11, 2001.[12]

While the group may seem to be led by radicals, there is a definite superficial mainstream streak to this group, which makes it all the more dangerous. In the mid-1990s, its president was Linda Darling-Hammond, who served as the head of President-elect Barack Obama's education policy working group in 2008. She is still very active in AERA.

After this book proves to be a little skunk at the left's garden party, I'm not holding my breath waiting to receive an invitation to its next pointy-headed soirée.

California Federation of Teachers

In the fall of 1987, the leaders of the California Federation of Teachers were alarmed that "the new generation of teachers lacked a basic understanding not only of the origins of their rights, but also of the centrality of union activism for maintaining—let alone extending—those rights," according to the book "Organizing the Curriculum" (see more in chapter 21).

The union created the "Labor in the Schools Committee," which has a two-fold task: "Educating the CFT's members about their own history, as well as the history of the broader labor movement; and educating K-12 students about the role and contributions of unions and the labor movement to American society," according to the book.

The lesson plans, videos and other materials generated and promoted by this committee seem to be the most pervasive of any union-based activist group.

Members of the committee, as of August 2011, include:

- Don Brown, Pajaro Valley Federation of Teachers
- Jeanie Brown, Santa Cruz Council of Classified Employees
- Jose Colon, Berkeley Federation of Teachers
- Tom Edminster, United Educators of San Francisco
- Richard Hathaway, ABC Federation of Teachers
- Ann Holliday, Coast Federation of Educators
- Teresa Laughlin, Palomar Faculty Federation
- Anne Mayer, AFT College Staff Guild
- Kelly Mayhew, AFT Guild-San Diego Community Colleges
- Jim Miller, AFT Guild-San Diego Community Colleges
- Phil Moore, Salinas Valley Federation of Teachers
- Bill Morgan, United Educators of San Francisco
- Luz Nunez, AFT College Staff
- Sheri Pavelka, United Teachers Los Angeles
- Ken Roberts, AFT College Staff Guild
- Linda Tubach, United Teachers Los Angeles
- Fred Glass, Staff Liaison
- Ed Wang, Staff Liaison[13]

New York Collective of Radical Educators (NYCoRE)

This is how NYCoRE describes itself on its website:

> "New York Collective of Radical Educators (NYCoRE) is a group of public school educators committed to fighting for social justice in our school system and society at large, by organizing and mobilizing teachers, developing curriculum, and working with community, parent, and student organizations. We are educators who believe that education is an integral part of social change and that we

must work both inside and outside the classroom because the struggle for justice does not end when the school bell rings."[14]

Besides developing the Social Justice Plan Book (see Chapter 11), and the illegal immigration and racist cookie lessons, the group also holds an annual conference for its members. Bill Ayers was its 2011 keynote speaker.[15] (Is there anything he *doesn't* do?)

At the same conference—themed "Whose Schools? Our Schools!"—group leader Bree Picower told the audience, "We organize for justice both within our classrooms in terms of the curriculum and outside our classrooms in terms of different social actions that we take around educational issues."[16]

Teachers for Social Justice

A group of Chicago progressives, called "Teachers for Social Justice," holds an annual curriculum fair. *Lawndale for Justice News*—which appears to be a student-run media outlet—covered the 10th annual fair which was held in November 2010.

Justice News interviewed Chicago Teachers Union Chief of Staff Jackson Potter, who described "Teachers for Social Justice" as an "organization of primarily educators—both elementary, high school and college—who believe that what they teach should be based in improving the world and the communities where they teach."

> "It's both locally in your own community, so if there's [*sic*] injustices happening—the power plant in Little Village, for example, that's polluting the air and making people have asthma—that would be something you should learn about in your classroom; how to deal with those problems and the science behind it. Globally, you can think about why are certain countries having to be the repository for all the garbage the United States creates. We're 5 percent of the population but we produce 25 percent of the garbage and take 25 percent of the resources. Those types of questions

are the types of questions T4SJ thinks you should learn about in the classroom."[17]

At the risk of getting into fact-checking—and I'm no physician—I must point out that pollution doesn't "create" asthma. Children are born with it. While air contaminants certainly don't help, they don't *create* asthma. He must be reading the same junk science studies as President Obama.[18]

Secondly, who forces any country to be "the repository" for American garbage? A few years ago, a huge legislative fight erupted in Michigan because the state was a repository for Canadian garbage! It was such a kerfuffle, it led to Michigan being nicknamed the "great waste state."

So, according to Potter, students should be learning junk science and bad information, which seems to be the central mission of the Teachers for Social Justice.

Justice News also interviewed Jon Reitzel, a math teacher at—no joke—Social Justice High School. He said:

> "In our current unit, we're going to be looking at mathematics of student loans, of credit card loans, of mortgage loans, about how a larger system of a capitalistic nature of our country affects people and how if they knew a little bit more information—if they knew a little bit more about how these systems worked—that maybe they can better counter them and suggest a different way—so that the world could change. 'A new world is possible, a new education is necessary,' so that theme can go through classes and I come here to be reenergized and reminded that there's important work that needs to be done."[19]

At the 2009 Teachers for Social Justice fair, a representative of the "Association of Raza Educators – California" told attendees, "It's all about collectivism, it's all about collective struggle, it's better, especially if you feel that you're overwhelmed—it's about a family unit—it's about us, it's not about me."[20]

A girl with "Chicago Youth Initiating Change" told the audience:

> "We want to create revolution for liberation in education. We are tired of learning about rich white people history. We want to learn something real that relates to us, our people and our struggles and our history . . . We are down for the struggle, are you?"[21]

Masters of their domain

Critics of this book will likely say that I've only picked out a handful of teachers, out of the more than three million in American schools, and these are just the worst examples. But these are just the teachers we know about. Some of these lessons are more pervasive than others. Some, like "The Story of Stuff," have gone so mainstream, that several schools actually post a link to the video right on their school's homepage.

And many of the activist teachers feel the classroom is their exclusive domain. They seem to believe that taxpayers and parents—who actually provide the resources for the whole bloated behemoth to operate—are somehow intruding on their territory. Just look at the response from the defenders of the status quo when the system is challenged. The typical response reformers get is, "Have you ever taught in a classroom?" As if the customer has no right—no authority—to question how things are being run.

Bernard Gassaway, a former school principal in New York City, summarized the prevailing attitude in many public schools in a 2006 column. He said schools often treat parents as if they should mind their own business:

> "School business is for educators, not parents. Parents need to focus more on raising their children than getting too involved in what goes on in schools . . . As harsh as this may sound, this is an expressed sentiment among many educators across this country in both public and private school systems. I have heard this from colleagues, and I have experienced it as a parent."[22]

Parents often feel they're an inconvenience to administrators, teachers and "the system." But the reality is *we* own it. And oftentimes, the problems seem so ingrained and expansive, they seem overwhelming for parents who often feel alone in their struggle to improve their local schools.

CHAPTER 37

What *You* Can Do

Many parents and taxpayers believe the problems in public education are overwhelming for one person and there is nothing they can do. The truth is that there are several things individuals can do to make a difference. In Education Action Group's documentary series, "Kids Aren't Cars," we laid out many of the problems and some of the solutions.[23]

Ultimately, parents own their children's education. Not school boards. Not other politicians. Not teachers and definitely not bureaucrats. None of those people will move a muscle until they feel heat. The reality is the establishment will not change until it is more afraid of parents than it is of the teachers' unions. The unions hold the power and sway. Therefore, parents need to get pushy.

Property owners and goods purchasers pay thousands of dollars a year for public education. We're paying for the system, we own it and we should have more of a say how it operates. Like any monopoly, it's going to take a lot to force change. But to get the monopoly to begin grinding its rusty change gears, a little healthy competition needs to be injected into the system.

But, of course, the monopoly will resist any competition. It will throw out ridiculous reasons for why parents shouldn't have options. It will pull fast ones, like it did in Toledo, Ohio.

It is state law in Ohio that when a public school district decides to close a school, the empty buildings must first be offered for sale to other schools (i.e. charter schools).[24] But fearing competition, the Toledo school board ignored that little inconvenience and added a deed restriction while trying to sell one of its unused buildings: The property could not be used for a charter school. What a convenient way to hamper the competition.

This is what a scared, vulnerable monopoly that fears competition does.

But what, if any, was the reaction from the public? Except for a few talk radio hosts, like *WSPD's* Brian Wilson, not much. Blogger Maggie Thurber covered it expertly.[25] But parents were largely mute. Parents failed to speak up and the establishment won again.

What follows are some suggested points of action parents, taxpayers and elected officials can take.

Parents

I.   What is being taught?

Parents are the customers of the educational service. Own it. Demand only the best.

Do you know what texts and materials are being used? What is the ideological persuasion of the teacher? Is he or she pushing leftist propaganda through the back door?

Rachael Proctor, the mother of a 1st grader in Cordova, Tennessee, heard her daughter singing a strange song one day and asked her about it. Here's how Proctor described it during an April 2011 interview on *Fox News*:

> "She came home from school two weeks ago and I was on the phone with a friend and she started singing this song and she got to that part about don't drive in your car by yourself, don't buy plastic, boycott, petition the big business and I literally stopped dead in my tracks and I asked her, 'Can you please sing that for mommy one more time?' I wanted to make sure I was hearing her right."[26]

The song was "Earth Day Rap" by Doug Goodkin. Here are the lyrics:

> The sky is high and the ocean is deep
> But we can't treat the planet like a garbage heap
> Don't wreck it, protect it, keep part of it wild
> And think about the future of your great-grandchild
> Recycle, bicycle, don't you drive by yourself
> Don't buy those plastic products on the supermarket shelf
> Boycott, petition, let the big business know
> That if we mess it up here, there's nowhere else to go
> Don't shrug your shoulders, say, "What can I do?"
> Only one person can do it and that person is you![27]

Proctor and her husband then contacted the school principal to get some answers.

> ". . . We kindly asked that she would pull the song from the program as they were singing some other songs in celebration of Earth Day and she told us the song was cute, the kids enjoyed singing it, they don't understand, the song doesn't mean what I think it does, it comes out of a state-approved text book, so she would not pull the song."[28]

Proctor told *Fox & Friends* that the school allowed her daughter not to participate in the program. She helped with the curtain instead.

These situations put parents and students in awkward spots because it's intimidating and embarrassing to take a stand. But parents with children in public schools must decide if they're going to have them participate in these indoctrination activities, or if they're going to do some educating of their own. Proctor is one who chose the latter.

II. Look at all of your schooling options.

Do you know what types of schools are in your neighborhood or community? Do you know how they perform? Do you have virtual schooling options? Do you have the capacity to home school?

There are many options that are potentially available to you. Some parents are fortunate enough to have access to a voucher program. Everyone has a traditional public school option, but is there a local charter school? Private and parochial schools? A virtual school? Do your homework. A good place to start is with the Education Breakthrough Network (www. EdBreakThrough.org).

Oftentimes, charter schools hold a lottery because the number of applicants often exceeds the number of seats available. Lotteries typically occur in the late winter or early spring—before you may be thinking about schooling options.

Participate in an exciting time in January: National School Choice Week. Reform advocates of every political stripe come together to increase options for parents (SchoolChoiceWeek.com).

It is incumbent upon parents to own their child's education. No one else will.

III.   Get to know your child's teacher.

Prior to enrolling in a school, request to meet the teacher in your child's classroom. Perhaps even ask to observe the teacher during the school day. This will give you a good indication as to the environment you will be putting your child in.

Once you select a school, interact with the teacher. Don't be a nit-picking bother, but just stay engaged with the educational process. Stay tuned into what is being taught. Are the things covered in the preceding chapters also in your classroom? Are there behavioral or academic performance issues?

IV.   Find out if your child attends a student-focused school.

Many public schools have a snappy, upbeat mission statement on their website, but sometimes their actions don't back it up. Far too many schools have damaged relations between administrators and teachers, the union and the school board or any combination thereof.

As a negotiating tactic to gain leverage on the school board, some unions will declare a "work rule"—that is, they will only do what is specifically spelled out in the contract. That can produce serious, tangible consequences for parents and students. The union hopes this strategy will upset parents and students and entice them into putting pressure on the school board.

For example, a group of Michigan teachers refused to help with an in-school store that sold paper, pens and other supplies to generate revenue for the post-graduation Senior Night. Why? Because it wasn't in the contract and the school board wasn't meeting the union's demands at the bargaining table.

In southern New Jersey, teachers refused to write letters of recommendation for students seeking admission to universities. Why? Because it wasn't listed as a requirement in the contract and the unionized teachers wanted those students and parents to pressure the school board into settling a contract dispute in their favor.

This is ugly stuff. It's no way for organizations that purport to "put students first" to operate. But it happens every day and parents need to see right through it and hold the culprits accountable.

V. **If your neighborhood school is ineffective—or you see an ideological agenda being pushed, demand options from community and elected leaders.**

As I said earlier, until politicians and school board members are more afraid of parents than unions, nothing will change. If they don't hear from fed-up parents, they'll assume there is no problem. So if you aren't satisfied with the options you have, you need to speak up and tell everyone about it.

Taxpayers

The state of our public schools is not just a problem for parents. If you own property or pay sales tax, you're funding them. That means you have every right to know what's going on in the schools you are paying for. There are a variety of ways to do this.

VI.   Know your school board.

Who did the union endorse in the last election?

Are they calling for tax increases or spending reform?

If you're a taxpayer, parent or Tea Party group, interview school board candidates before the election and hold them accountable afterward.

Politicians are like water—they look for the path of least resistance. Unions have candidate recruitment and accountability down to a science. They publish manuals on the subject, right down to the wording of the candidate interview invitation letter. They're masters of pinning candidates down to positions and making them feel the union's wrath if they don't agree at the outset or stray from an established pro-union position. Very little of this is done by parents and taxpayer advocacy groups.

Many political candidates, hungry for elective office, seek union endorsements without knowing their true agenda. I have met candidates more conservative than myself that court the union, oblivious to the tiger they're about to catch by the tail. But they seek the endorsement of "the teachers"—those in the trenches, fighting for what's best for our children—and the campaign contribution and sway that comes along with it.

VI.   If you don't like what's happening, run for the school board. Contact American Majority for training at www. AmericanMajority.org.

I have met countless candidates who have convinced themselves they will be successful on Election Day, only to get slaughtered. Some have told me about supposed "polling" that showed them well-positioned to win, but when the vote came around, they lost. Big time.

There are fundamentals of a campaign that cannot be overlooked, regardless of how new and innovative you think your ideas are. But this is the time for reform-minded parents and taxpayers to stand up, quit complaining and get involved. The Tea Party movement has been an invaluable development for fiscal accountability and transparency. At the events I've been invited to speak at, average people have come up to me saying it was the first time they took a political stand outside of voting. It has awakened hundreds of thousands, if not millions, of people to the way their government operates.

But attending a rally doesn't enact change. Holding a position of power does.

VII.   Look into how your public school is spending YOUR money. It's not their money—it's your money.

Elected politicians, whether at the school board or state level, hold the purse strings to billions of our tax dollars dedicated to educating our children. Do you know how they're being spent? Does your school board voluntarily post spending information on its website? The Mackinac Center for Public Policy (mackinac.org) in Michigan began publicizing which school districts were posting their check registries online. In some instances, that strategy shamed the schools into doing the right thing. Suddenly, the public saw the thousands of dollars that were being spent on floral arrangements and underground sprinkling contracts. Sunlight remains the best disinfectant. Demand that it shines in your school district.

VIII.   Demand to know what is going on in contract negotiations.

While school board members are elected to represent taxpayers—and theoretically *our* interests—oftentimes they become a part of the establishment and can grow hostile to questioning.

As such, they like to keep critical, grueling details from the public until it's too late. Specifically, the public is often shut out of the contract negotiation process until after the contract is ratified by the school board and the local teachers union. At that point, it's too late to question a particular concession made by a school board because the signatures are affixed and it carries the weight of law.

Some school boards are beginning to open up negotiations to the public. Not the lengthy session themselves, but some are posting proposals and counter-proposals for the taxpaying public to see.

This usually infuriates union leaders because many of their demands, which are typically made behind closed doors, are expensive, unsustainable and not based in reality.

Again, sunlight is the best disinfectant. When the union knows the public can view its list of insane, if not offensive, demands, they're usually not made. And if they are, the union runs the risk of alienating other (albeit private sector) union members that have given concessions to help their employers through difficult financial times.

Elected Officials

IX. Give parents options.

Politicians should do whatever they can to help students escape chronically failing public schools. But I revert back to my previous statement: Politicians are oftentimes more afraid of unions than they are of parents. And unions hate competition from alternative schools. Until that changes, don't expect more options.

X. Consider a Parent Trigger law, as California's Parent Revolution did.

The Parent Trigger law should be replicated in every single community in America. Do we own the schools or do they own us? If parents care enough to try to fix their kids' school, shouldn't they be allowed to?

We constantly hear from the education establishment that parents need to be more involved.

Here's the establishment's opportunity to put actions behind their words: Support a parent trigger law in each state and let parents really get involved.

XI. Stand with U.S. Sen. Joe Lieberman (I-CT) in believing that students trapped in failing schools should be rescued immediately, by any means necessary. Refuse to wait for bureaucrats to tinker with the system.

There are many things about which Sen. Lieberman and I disagree, but I think he is one of the most upstanding members of Congress. On the issue of school choice, there's no daylight between us. He is spot on when it comes to school choice and education reform. Lieberman, a Democrat-turned-Independent, even took the bold move of standing up to the NEA and telling the union it was deceiving the public regarding the effectiveness of the D.C. Opportunity Scholarship Program.

He has a reasonable compromise: Don't force students to languish in failing schools while the pointy-headed bureaucrats assemble turn-around plans and tinker with the system. Give those kids a way out. Now.

XII.   Increase transparency.

If public education is the flawless system the establishment makes it out to be, it can withstand any amount of scrutiny. Instead, much of the business is kept from the public. Taxpayers have to fight for more transparency. Legislators have to mandate it. School districts should (albeit painfully) level with the citizens about their performance and student success—or lack thereof. Sleights of hand and dishonesty hurt no one but the students—the people the establishment says it cares about the most.

XIII. Post financial data online.

School districts should voluntarily post easy-to-understand budgets and spending data online. My local school district publishes basic pie charts. Because of that, I know that it spends 26% of its budget on health insurance benefits. I think such expenses are outrageous—if not criminal—but kudos to district leaders for having the guts to put it out there.

Post a check registry so taxpayers can see where the dollars are going. If school leaders believe every dollar is well-spent, and there really truly is a need for more, taxpayers will draw that conclusion themselves with the proper information. If they believe basic information is being kept from them, that's when they turn on school leaders.

XIV.   Be forthcoming about teacher effectiveness.

Schools need to have a fair system for evaluating teachers, and that data needs to be made public. We owe it to our students to have a quality, effective teacher in front of every classroom in America. We're paying too much to receive anything less.

Public evaluations are not an attempt to belittle or demean anyone; they are meant to show the public the quality of school employees it has. Take the cue from other school employees—if they won't put their child in a certain teacher's classroom, no one else should be expected to, either.

XV.   Reform/Eliminate tenure and "last hired, first fired" policies.

Tenure—which protects teachers from being easily fired—has no place at the K-12 level. Curriculum is pretty well defined by a school board or state board and teachers have to live within fairly strict parameters (except when they stray into the indoctrination garbage I covered earlier). In other words, K-12 teachers don't need tenure protection for the purposes of ensuring academic freedom. Tenure protects bad teachers who don't deserve it.

And the idea of school administrators flipping a coin at layoff time to see who stays and who goes is insane, but that's what many teacher contracts stipulate. It's an insult to hard-working, effective teachers who are dedicated to students. Simply because they haven't been there as long as the next guy shouldn't mean they're out of a job. It's not right.

XVI. End the conflict of interest and money-making schemes by organized labor that are distractions and create unnecessary fights in our communities.

Some unions—such as the Michigan Education Association—have set up health care entities that provide health benefits to school employees on the school district's dime. Those entities then pay the union a fee for "marketing" its insurance at contract negotiation time.[29] In layman's terms, it's a kickback provided to the union. It's a money-making scheme. Moreover, it represents a power mechanism for the union because, time and time again, the union trots MESSA out to its members as an example of the stellar work it's doing for them.

With schemes like this, suddenly union priorities are skewed: Does the union keep its highly-priced health plan for teachers and risk more layoffs, or does it sacrifice healthcare kickbacks to keep more dues payers on the job? It's a conundrum that is impacting schools and communities.

I say that because we often see very ugly fights during contract negotiation time about issues that have no impact on student learning.

You have your instructions

Parents must control the educational process. "The system" won't look out for your child. Only you can. Far too many parents cede control and oversight to a system that is fundamentally flawed.

We must each do what we can to fix the education system. Clearly those involved can't be trusted to do it or they would have by now.

I want to hear your stories. Please find me on Facebook (facebook.com/kyleolson4) or email me at kyolson4@gmail.com. You are a crucial player in taking our schools back and keeping America exceptional.

Acknowledgements

Thank you to my wife and boys—you are the reason I get up every morning and fight the good fight. You are saints for tolerating my workaholism and travel.

Thanks to Dick Morris for being one of the first people to believe in me and the mission of Education Action Group—and for expecting nothing in return. What an honor it is to have you involved in this effort.

Thanks to Andrew Breitbart for having the courage to take the fight directly to the enemies of American exceptionalism. You have given so many conservatives courage, a voice and a platform.

Thanks to the many supporters of EAG. The initial funders who believed in us when we had no track record—you're the reason we are where we are today.

Thank you to the parents, teachers and reform activists we've worked with along the way. Our kids need more people like all of you.

Thank you to my parents, who lead lives of honesty, commitment, hard work and dedication. Dad, you are the living definition of the North Star—you're honest, trustworthy and the model of what a businessman should be. And you have always put your family first. When a falter, I look to you for how I should be.

Thanks to my grandparents and the rest of the Greatest Generation. May we draw on your inspiration to once again defeat America's enemies. This time, they're within our own borders. I bet my grandfather never would have thought his machinists union would come to support the "useful idiots."

Thanks to Bob Dylan for being an original and doing it your way. I hope I can do the same.

Thank you to my loyal and much-loved companions at EAG. It's an honor to be in the trenches with you.

Thank you to the wealthy Americans who are so demonized by leftists, but give their resources so children can receive a better education. You exemplify the best of America. You don't accept the status quo or an education system that unions have *had* the power to change but have been unwilling. You give voice to the thousands of parents who don't have one.

I sometimes wonder if they hate you so much because you're trying to lift their clientele out of poverty and hopelessness.

And thank you for reading this book and considering my perspective.

Endnotes

(Note: All web-based sources were current as of August 2011.)

Introduction

1. Dr. Theodore Baehr and Pat Boone, <u>The Culture-Wise Family: Upholding Christian Values in a Mass-Media World</u> (Venture, CA: Regal Books, 2007).

2. Wendy Owen, *Hillsboro School Board stirs up controversy about 'winter break' versus 'Christmas break'*, http://www.oregonlive.com/hillsboro/index. ssf/2011/04/hillsboro_school_board_stirs_up_controversy_about_winter_ break_versus_christmas_break.html.

3. Stephanie Klein, *Seattle school renames Easter eggs 'Spring Spheres'*, http:// mynorthwest. com /?nid=11&sid=459668.

4. Seattle.gov, *Events Calendar*, http://www.seattle.gov/parks/calendar/? trumbaEmbed=date %3D20110423.

5. Brock Parker, *School system to get Muslim holiday*, http://www.boston. com/news/education/k_12/articles/2010/10/10/school_system_ to_get_muslim_holiday/?page=full.

6. Kerry Picket, *NYC school teacher: Here's how you promote socialism in the classroom*, http://www.washingtontimes.com/blog/watercooler/2011/apr/21/ video-nyc-school-teacher-heres-how-you-promote-soc/.

7. William S. Lind, "Who Stole Our Culture," in <u>The Culture-Wise Family: Upholding Christian Values in a Mass-Media World</u>, ed. Dr. Theodore Baehr and Pat Boone, (Venture, CA: Regal Books, 2007), 178-185.

8. Rachel Gillespie, *Do you think teens know the difference between Madison and Marx?*, http://blog.billofrightsinstitute.org/2010/12/do-you-think-teens- know-the-difference-between-madison-and-marx/.

9. Rochelle Riley, *Reading gives DPS grad voice and choice in life*, http://www. freep.com /article/20100205/COL10/2050352/Reading-gives-DPS-grad- voice-choice-life.

10. Education Action Group, *Kids Aren't Cars: An Epic Failure —Detroit, Part 2*, http://www.youtube.com/watch?v=ZugKnWB8s1E&feature=player_ embedded#!.

How Teachers Spread Cultural Marxism

1. Wisconsin Labor History Society, *Governor signs historic labor in the schools bill*, http://www. wisconsinlaborhistory.org/?p=265.

2. Sen. Mark Leno, *FAIR Education Act (SB 48) fact sheet*, http://www.eqca. org/atf/cf/ %7B34f258b3-8482-4943-91cb-08c4b0246a88%7D/FAIR%20 EDUCATION%20FACT%20SHEET%20 FINAL.PDF.

3. Targeted News Service, *State of California Newsletter for Friday July 15, 2011*, http:// targetednews.com/nl_disp.php?nl_date_id=241632.

4. Southern California Public Radio, *SB 48 adds a new LGBT chapter to California history textbooks*, http://www.scpr.org/programs/patt-morrison/2011/07/06/19777/california-textbooks-to-include-lgbt-information.

5. Sahil Kapur, *California passes bill to counteract 'disturbing' Texas curriculum*, http://www.rawstory.com/rs/2010/05/30/california-disturbing-texas-curriculum/.

6. Education Reporter, *Maryland students must be 'green' to graduate*, http:// www.eagleforum.org/educate/2011/july11/green-to-graduate.html.

7. Maryland State Department of Education, *Programs: State Regulations*, http:// www.marylandpublicschools.org/MSDE/programs/environment/info/ regulations.htm.

8. Bert Bower and Jim Lobdell, <u>Social Studies Alive! Our Community and Beyond</u>, (Palo Alto, CA: Teachers' Curriculum Institute, 2003).

9. Ibid., 104-105.

10. Ibid., 102-103.

11. Ibid., 130-131.

12. Robert McCartney, *Biased 3rd-grade book's goals admirable, but Frederick shouldn't use it*, http://www.washingtonpost.com/local/frederick-shouldnt -use-slanted-3rd-grade-textbook—even-if-it-leans-same-way-i-do/2011/07/06/gIQAJVpC1H_story.html.

13. Melissa Jenco, *Parent fighting perceived liberal bias in textbook*, http://triblocal. com/st-charles/2011/07/27/parent-fighting-perceived-liberal-bias-in-textbook/.

14. Jeff Ward, *Taking exception to gripes about social studies text*, http://couriernews. suntimes.com/news/talk/6771306-418/taking-exception-to-gripes-about-social-studies-text.html.

15. NYSUT Media Relations, *Speak Truth to Power human rights curriculum launched in New York*, http://www.nysut.org/cps/rde/xchg/nysut/hs.xsl/mediareleases_15938.htm.

16. Speak Truth to Power, *The Curriculum*, http://blogs.nysut.org/sttp/curriculum/.

17. New York Times, *New York School Test Scores: Chestnut Ridge Middle School*, http://projects.nytimes.com/new-york-schools-test-scores/counties/rockland/districts/east-ramapo-central-school-district-spring-valley/schools/chestnut-ridge-middle-school.

18. Speak Truth to Power, *Van Jones: Police Brutality*, http://blogs.nysut.org/sttp/2010/11/09/ van-jones-police-brutality/.

19. YouTube, *NEA Delegate Meeting*, http://www.youtube.com/watch?v=aZh08-u0Dg.

20. Lola Adesioye, *After Oscar Grant, just take guns away from US police officers*, http://www. guardian.co.uk/commentisfree/cifamerica/2010/jul/09/oscar-grant-shooting-us-police.

21. Ellen Wolpert, "Rethinking 'The Three Little Pigs,'" in <u>Rethinking Our Classrooms: Teaching for Equity and Justice, vol. 1</u>, ed. Wayne Au, Bill Bigelow and Stan Karp (Milwaukee: Rethinking Schools, 2007), 8.

22. Lindsay Lamb, Rebecca Bigler, Lynn Liben and Vanessa Green, *Gender doesn't limit you: A research-based anti-bullying program for the early grades*, http://www.tolerance.org/sites/default/ files/general/tt_gender_doesnt_limit-2.pdf.

23. National Assessment of Educational Progress, *NAEP Questions, Pre-Algebra, Unit 06B: Probability*, http://rpdp.net/adm/uploads/math/2311PreAlgebra Unit06B.11A.11BNAEPQuestions Probability.pdf.

24. Everyday Just Living, *Nothing sweet about cocoa beans picked by slaves*, http://bambootique.wordpress.com/2008/04/28/nothing-sweet-about-cocoa-beans-picked-by-slaves/.

25. Jonathan Osler, *A Guide for Integrating Issues of Social and Economic Justice into Mathematics Curriculum (a work in progress)*, http://www.radicalmath.org/docs/SJMathGuide.pdf.

26. National Assessment of Educational Progress, *The Nation's Report Card—Mathematics 2009: National Assessment of Educational Progress at Grades 4 and 8*, http://nces.ed.gov/nationsreport card/pdf/main2009/2010451.pdf.

27. Stokely Carmichael, "Berkeley Speech," in <u>Contemporary American Voices: Significant Speeches in American History, 1945—Present</u>, ed. James R. Andrews and David Zarefsky, (New York: Longman Publishing Group, 1992), 100-107.

28. Tom Larson, Sam Bernstein and Steve Leigh, *Time to take from the banks and give to schools*, http://www.www.socialistworker.org/2011/06/08/take-from-banks-and-give-to-schools.

29. Wayne Au, '*What We Want, What We Believe': Teaching with the Black Panthers' Ten Point Program*, http://zinnedproject.org/posts/170.

30. Wayne Au, "'What We Want, What We Believe': Teaching with the Black Panthers' Ten Point Program," <u>Rethinking Schools</u> 16, no. 1 (Fall 2001).

31. Sam Dillon, *U.S. Students Remain Poor at History, Tests Show*, http://www.nytimes.com/ 2011/06/15/education/15history.html?_r=2.

32. Brian Bolduc, *Don't Know Much About History*, http://online.wsj.com/article/SB100014240 52702304432304576369421525987128.html.

33. Ibid.

34. Bill Bigelow, "Teaching about Unsung Heroes: Encouraging students to appreciate those who fought for social justice," in <u>Rethinking Our Classrooms: Teaching for Equity and Justice, vol. 2</u>, ed. Bill Bigelow, Brenda Harvey, Stan Karp and Larry Miller (Milwaukee: Rethinking Schools, 2001), 37-41.

35. Howard Zinn, "Unsung Heroes," in <u>Rethinking Our Classrooms: Teaching for Equity and Justice, vol. 2</u>, ed. Bill Bigelow, Brenda Harvey, Stan Karp and Larry Miller (Milwaukee: Rethinking Schools, 2001), 35-36.

36. Ray Raphael, "Re-examining the Revolution," <u>Rethinking Schools</u> 19, no. 2 (Winter 2004/05).

37. MYFOXNY.COM, *Shame, Shame, Shame: Racist Cookies in 'Honor' of Barack Obama*, http://www.myfoxny.com/dpp/news/090122_Racist_Cookies_in_Honor_of_Barack_Obama.

38. Education for Liberation Network, *Beat it! Defeat it! Racist Cookies! We Won't Eat it!*, http://www.edliberation.org/resources/records/beat-it-defeat-it-racist-cookies-we-wont-eat-it/view.

39. Beth Fertig, *Drop-Out Rate May Be Higher Than Reported, Audit Shows*, http://www.wnyc.org/blogs/wnyc-news-blog/2011/mar/29/state-audit-questions-city-graduation-and-dropout-rates/.

40. *Agreement between the Board of Education of the Grand Rapids Public Schools and the Grand Rapids Education Association*, http://www.mackinac.org/archives/epi/contracts/41010_2011-8-20_GREA_E.pdf.

41. Tara Mack and Bree Picower, eds., <u>Planning to Change the World: A Plan Book for Social Justice Teachers, 2011-2012</u>, (New York: New York Collective of Radical Educators and the Education Liberation Network, 2011), 3.

42. Southern Poverty Law Center, *Teaching Tolerance: F is for Fair!*, http://www.tolerance.org/ activity/f-fair.

43. Southern Poverty Law Center, *Teaching Tolerance: What do Halloween costumes say?*, http://www.tolerance.org/activity/what-do-halloween-costumes-say.

Save the Whales by Killing Capitalism

1. Frank Beckmann, *'Sustainable' curriculum teaches kids to envy success*, http://www.publicschoolspending.com/wp-content/uploads/2011/07/Creative-Change-Detroit-News-article.pdf.

2. http://www.publicschoolspending.com/wp-content/uploads/2011/07/Creative-Change-Eastover-Elementary-invoice.pdf.

3. http://www.publicschoolspending.com/wp-content/uploads/2011/07/Creative-Change-Consulting-Agreement-with-Ann-Arbor-Public-Schools.pdf.

4. http://www.publicschoolspending.com/wp-content/uploads/2011/07/Creative-Change-Educational-Vendor-Invoice.pdf.

5. Creative Change Educational Solutions, *Economics for the Common Good*, http://www. creativechange.net/programs/economics.

6. Leslie Kaufman, *A cautionary video about America's 'stuff'*, http://www.nytimes.com/2009 /05/11/education/11stuff.html?pagewanted=1&_r=1&hp.

7. Rory Cooper, *The Story of Lies: Greenpeace in Your Kid's School*, http://blog.heritage.org/2009/05/11/the-story-of-lies-greenpeace-in-your-kids-school/.

8. http://www.publicschoolspending.com/daily-updates/annie-leonard-story-of-stuff-balle-2010-speech/.

9. Carroll County Public School, *Curriculum and Instruction: Elementary School*, http://carrollk12.org/instruction/instruction/stem/elementary/default.asp.

10. T.T. Minor Elementary School, *Homepage*, http://olive.seattleschools.org/schools/tt_minor/.

11. Current.com, *What is the story of stuff?*, http://current.com/news-and-politics/89521363_what-is-the-story-of-stuff.htm.

12. Dominic Berbeo, *Pledge to the Earth proposed for council*, http://www.publicschoolspending.com/wp-content/uploads/2011/06/LACouncilPledgeproposed.pdf.

13. Rick Orlov, *Padilla hopes colleagues won't bite hand that feeds them*, http://www.publicschoolspending.com/wp-content/uploads/2011/06/LACouncilPledgetotheEarthburied.pdf.

14. White Oaks PTA, *White Oaks Acorn*, http://www.publicschoolspending.com/wp-content/uploads/2011/06/June_2010_Acorn.pdf.

15. Rosalie Tyler Paul, '*I pledge allegiance to the Earth*', http://www.timesrecord.com/articles/2011/04/15/opinion/commentaries/doc4da86e40a157d487996360.txt.

16. Valerie Strauss, *Matt Damon's clear-headed speech to teachers rally*, http://www.washingtonpost.com/blogs/answer-sheet/post/matt-damons-clear-headed-speech-to-teachers-rally/2011/07/30/gIQAG9Q6jI_blog.html.

17. Jana Dean, "Teaching about Global Warming in Truck Country," in <u>Rethinking Our Classrooms: Teaching for Equity and Justice, vol. 1</u>, ed. Bill Bigelow, Linda Christensen, Stan Karp, Barbara Miner and Bob Peterson (Milwaukee: Rethinking Schools, 2007), 57-67.

18. Jonathan Osler, *A Guide for Integrating Issues of Social and Economic Justice into Mathematics Curriculum (a work in progress)*, http://www.radicalmath.org/docs/SJMathGuide.pdf.

19. YouTube, *Bertha Lewis Sings—Walmart Sucks!*, http://www.youtube.com/watch?v=-axx7tEiHNc.

20. Amy Standen, *Big Box Stores*, http://www.ecologycenter.org/tfs/pdf/2005summer/ Big_Box_Stores.pdf.

21. Ibid.

22. Southern Poverty Law Center, *Teaching Tolerance: Introducing Kids to the Idea of Environmental Racism*, http://www.tolerance.org/activity/introducing-kids-idea-environmental-raci.

23. Jesse Finfrock, *Q&A: Van Jones*, http://motherjones.com/environment/2008/10/qa-van-jones.

24. Bill Morgan and the Labor in the Schools Committee of the California Federation of Teachers, *I, Tomato*, http://www.cft.org/uploads/LIS/i%20tomato.pdf.

<u>Unions Cultivate Solidarity in the Classroom</u>

1. Adelphi University, *Education & Labor Collaborative*, http://education.adelphi.edu/edulc /rationale_goals.php.

2. Rob Linné, "Introduction," in <u>Organizing the Curriculum: Perspectives on Teaching the US Labor Movement</u>, ed. Rob Linné, Leigh Benin and Adrienne Sosin (Rotterdam: Sense Publishers, 2009), xi—xiv.

3. Southern Poverty Law Center, *Teaching Tolerance: Labor Matters*, http://www.tolerance.org /activity/labor-matters.

4. James Parks, *Get Last-Minute Gifts at the Union Shop Online*, http://blog.aflcio.org/2009/ 12/12/get-last-minute-gifts-at-the-union-shop-online/.

5. Mary Eggebraaten, *Literary Lesson Plan*, http://buildingamerica.pbworks.com/w/page/37995605/Big%20Annie-Click,%20Clack%20Moo%20Lesson.

6. Michelle Anthony, *Click, Clack, Moo: Electric Blanket Science*, http://teachers.net/lessons/ posts/3349.html.

7. Kati Gilson, *Explaining to students why unions matter*, http://www.ctunet.com/media/chicago-union-teacher/downloadable-pdf/CUT-2011-06-10-web.pdf.

8. Phyllis Chiu, *Trouble in the Hen House*, http://www.cft.org/uploads/LIS/trouble%20in% 20the%20hen%20house.pdf.

9. John Kirk, *Board overrules arbitrator's decision!*, http://aft1493.org/advo/advo5-09.pdf.

10. Bob Peterson, "Why Teachers Should Know History: An Interview with Historian Howard Zinn," in <u>Transforming Teacher Unions: Fighting for Better Schools and Social Justice</u>, ed. Bob Peterson and Michael Charney (Milwaukee: Rethinking Schools, 1999), 76.

11. Kate Lyman, *Teaching and Learning in the Midst of the Wisconsin Uprising*, http://www. rethinkingschools.org/archive/25_04/25_04_lyman.shtml.

12. Ibid.

13. Dale Weiss, *Teaching Budget Cuts to Third Graders*, http://www.rethinkingschools.org/ archive/5_04/25_04_weiss.shtml.

14. Associated Press, *Milwaukee teachers fight for Viagra coverage*, http://www.cbsnews.com /stories/2010/08/06/health/main6748776.shtml.

15. California Federation of Teachers, *The Yummy Pizza Company: A Labor Studies Curriculum for Elementary Schools*, http://www.cft.org/uploads/LIS/yummy%20pizza%20company.pdf.

16. Margot Pepper, *Seven-year-olds lead a strike*, http://urbanhabitat.org/node/1196.

17. Linda Tubach and Patty Litwin, *Workplace Issues and Collective Bargaining in the Classroom*, http://zinnedproject.org/posts/4497.

18. YouTube, *UTLA teaches kids about collective bargaining*, http://www.youtube.com/watch? v=o66wh5KPqoA.

19. U.S. Department of Labor, *Union membership in California—2010*, http://www.bls.gov/ro9/ unionca.pdf.

20. YouTube, *UTLA teaches kids about collective bargaining*, http://www.youtube.com/watch? v=o66wh5KPqoA.

21. Linda Tubach, Patty Litwin and Ramon Cortines, *Inter-office correspondence*, http://www.publicschoolspending.com/wp-content/uploads/2011/06/prinicipals-CA.pdf

22. California Federation of Teachers, *California Labor History: Golden Lands, Working Hands*, http://www.cft.org/index.php/california-labor-history.html.

23. Michelle Vesecky, *Golden Lands, Working Hands: The History of the Future*, http://www.publicschoolspending.com/wp-content/uploads/2011/06/laborcenterreporter1994.pdf.

24. California Federation of Teachers, *View Golden Lands, Working Hands clips*, http://www. cft.org/index.php/california-labor-history/videos.html.

25. Brecht Forum, http://brechtforum.org/.

26. Frequently asked questions about unions, http://www.minneapolis1934.org/uploads /3/6/4/3/3643229/fred_glass_pdfs.pdf.

27. Michelle Vesecky, *Golden Lands, Working Hands: The History of the Future*, http://www.publicschoolspending.com/wp-content/uploads/2011/06/laborcenterreporter1994.pdf.

28. Bill Morgan and Bill Yund, *AutoWorks*, http://www.cft.org/uploads/LIS/autoworks.pdf.

29. William Bigelow and Norman Diamond, "Organic Goodie Simulation" in <u>The Power in Our Hands: A Curriculum on the History of Work and Workers in the United States</u>, ed. William Bigelow and Norman Diamond (New York: Monthly Review Press, 1988), 27-30.

30. Greg Queen, *Using Marx as the Fountainhead in Secondary Social Studies Curriculum Organization: A Rationale*, http://ted.coe.wayne.edu/sse/finding/queen.htm.

31. Clement Daly, *Thousands of Michigan teachers rally against education cuts*, http://www. wsws.org/articles/2010/jun2010/mich-j30.shtml.

Global Citizens: 'America' Is *Sooo* Last Century

1. The American Forum for Global Education, *Issues in Global Education: Issue No. 167 (2001-2002)*, http://www.globaled.org/issues/167.pdf.

2. Ibid.

3. World Concerns & the United Nations, *Equal Dignity and Worth Human Rights, Culture and Development, Grades 10-12 (ages 15-18)*, http://www. globaled.org/curriculum/UNE.html.

4. World Concerns & the United Nations, *More and Less, Grades 7-9 (ages 12-15)*, http://www. globaled.org/curriculum/UNC.html.

5. World Concerns & the United Nations, *Serving the World, Grades 7-9 (ages 12-15)*, http:// www.globaled.org/curriculum/UND.html.

6. World Concerns & the United Nations, *Serving the World at the International Level—a Role Play*, http://www.globaled.org/curriculum/UND-Reading-1. html.

7. World Concerns & the United Nations, *We Organize, Grades 4-6 (ages 9-12)*, http://www. globaled.org/curriculum/UNA.html.

8. Susan Hersh and Bob Peterson, "World Poverty and World Resources," in Rethinking Our Classrooms: Teaching for Equity and Justice, vol. 1, ed. Bill Bigelow, Linda Christensen, Stan Karp, Barbara Miner and Bob Peterson, (Milwaukee: Rethinking Schools, 2007), 103-105.

9. U.S. Grains Council, *Corn*, http://www.grains.org/corn.

10. New York Collective of Radical Educators, *No Human Is Illegal: An Educator's Guide for Addressing Immigration in the Classroom*, http://www.nycore.org/ newsite/wp-content/uploads/No-Human-Is-Illegal1.pdf.

11. Tara Mack and Bree Picower, eds., Planning to Change the World: A Plan Book for Social Justice Teachers, 2011-2012, (New York: New York Collective of Radical Educators and the Education Liberation Network, 2011), 44-45.

12. Marc Lacey, *Rift in Arizona as Latino Class Is Found Illegal*, http://www. nytimes.com/2011/01/08/us/08ethnic.html?_r=3&pagewanted=all.

13. Tara Mack and Bree Picower, eds., Planning to Change the World: A Plan Book for Social Justice Teachers, 2011-2012, (New York: New York Collective of Radical Educators and the Education Liberation Network, 2011), 44-45.

14. Marc Lacey, *Rift in Arizona as Latino Class Is Found Illegal*, http://www. nytimes.com /2011/01/08/us/08ethnic.html?_r=3&pagewanted=all.

15. MyFOXphoenix.com, *Students Protest Ethnic Studies Curriculum Change*, http://www.myfoxphoenix.com/dpp/news/education/students-protest-ethnic-studies-curriculum-change-4-26-11.

16. BBC, *Report challenges Haiti earthquake death toll*, http://www.bbc.co.uk/ news/world-us-canada-13606720.

17. Melissa Lafsky, *'Earthquakes Don't Kill People...Bad Buildings Do': More on Haiti's Building Codes*, http://www.infrastructurist.com/2010/01/20/earthquakes-dont-kill-peoplebad-buildings-do-more-on-haitis-building-codes/.

18.   Garrett Glass, *A Solution in Haiti: Try Freedom*, http://www.freerepublic. com/focus/f-news/2450857/posts.

19.   Walter Williams, *Haiti's Avoidable Death Toll*, http://www.jewishworldreview. com /cols/williams012010.php3.

20.   YouTube, *Mickey Mouse Goes to Haiti, Part 1*, http://www.youtube.com/ watch?v=6_OXhtgHBxk.

21.   Emma Rose Roderick, *Work, Workers & the U.S. Labor Movement Unit Plan for 5th grade Social Studies*, http://www.teachablemoment.org/elementary/ workers.html.

22.   "Daniel", *Christian Gamers Alliance Forums: Mickey Mouse Goes to Haiti*, http://www. cgalliance.org/forums/showthread.php?t=1446.

23.   The American Forum for Global Education, *Activity 8: The Sensible Use of the Shared Seas*, http://www.globaled.org/globalliteracy/activities/ glGlobalChallenges08.html.

24.   The American Forum for Global Education, *Diagram of the Seabed and the Ocean Floor Data*, http://www.globaled.org/globalliteracy/handouts/ glHandout08A.html.

Taking a Stand: Below-Average Purveyors of Classroom Marxism

1.   McKinsey & Company, *The Economic Impact of the Achievement Gap in America's Schools*, http://www.mckinsey.com/app_media/images/page_ images/offices/socialsector/pdf/achievement_gap_report.pdf.

2.   Ibid.

3.   McKinsey & Company, *Closing the Talent Gap: Attracting and Retaining Top-third Graduates to Careers in Teaching*, http://www.mckinsey.com/clientservice/ Social_Sector/our_practices/Education/ Knowledge_Highlights/~/media/ Reports/SSO/Closing_the_talent_gap.ashx.

4.   Vox Day, *Idiots at the chalkboard*, http://www.wnd.com/news/article. asp?ARTICLE_ID= 42742.

5.   Joy Resmovits, *Atlanta cheating scandal unveiled by reporters*, http:// www.huffingtonpost.com/2011/07/06/atlanta-public-schools- cheating_n_891737.html.

6.   Rethinking Schools, *About Rethinking Schools*, http://rethinkingschools.org/ about/index. shtml.

7.   Bill Bigelow and Bob Peterson, "'Is This Book Biased,'" in <u>Rethinking Globalization: Teaching for Justice in an Unjust World</u>, ed. Bill Bigelow and Bob Peterson (Milwaukee: Rethinking Schools, 2002), 5.

8. American Educational Research Association, *About AERA*, http://www.aera. net/AboutAERA. htm.

9. American Educational Research Association, *Social Justice Mission Statement*, http://www. aera.net/AboutAERA/Default.aspx?menu_id=90&id=1960.

10. The Well Spring, *AERA Social Justice in Education Award Recipient Bill Ayers*, http://www.curriculumstudies.net/storage/Div%20B%20Newsletter%20 2011.pdf.

11. William H. Schubert, *My friend and colleague, Bill Ayers*, http://theragblog. blogspot.com /2008/10/dr-william-h-schubert-bill-ayers-i-know.html.

12. Dinitia Smith, *No Regrets for a Love of Explosives; In a Memoir of Sorts, a War Protester Talks of Life With the Weathermen*, http://www.nytimes. com/2001/09/11/books/no-regrets-for-love-explosives-memoir-sorts-war-protester-talks-life-with.html.

13. California Federation of Teachers, *Labor in the Schools Committee*, http:// www.cft. org/index.php/committees/105.html.

14. New York Collective of Radical Educators, *Info*, http://www.nycore.org/ nycore-info/.

15. Vincent Muccioli, *NYCoRE 2011 Annual Conference Keynote Address*, http:// vimeo.com/ 22005999.

16. Grassroots Education Movement, *NYCoRE Conference: Whose Schools? Our Schools! Bill Ayers' Keynote*, http://vimeo.com/ 21552755.

17. YouTube, *The 10th Annual Teachers for Social Justice Curriculum Fair*, http:// www.youtube. com/watch?v=3EkXymtnFgI.

18. Matt Cover, *Obama Claims Air Pollution from Coal 'Creating Asthma for Kids Nearby'*, http://www.cnsnews.com/news/article/obama-claims-air-pollution-coal-creating.

19. YouTube, *The 10th Annual Teachers for Social Justice Curriculum Fair*, http:// www.youtube. com/watch?v=3EkXymtnFgI.

20. Teachers for Social Justice, *2009 Teaching for Social Justice Curriculum Fair Highlights*, http: //vimeo.com/8469375.

21. Ibid.

22. Bernard Gassaway, *Parents, Mind Your Own Business*, http://www. parentsunitedtogether. com/OwnBusiness.html.

23. Education Action Group, *Kids Aren't Cars and Our Schools Shouldn't Be Dropout Factories*, http://www.kidsarentcars.com/blog/.

24. LAWriter, *Ohio Laws and Rules: 3313.41 Disposal of real or personal property—acquisition of real property*, http://codes.ohio.gov/orc/3313.41.

25. Maggie Thurber, *UPDATED: Does Libbey HS deal violate state law?*, http://thurbersthoughts. blogspot.com/2011/04/does-libbey-hs-deal-violate-state-law.html.

26. Fox News, *Student Indoctrination to Honor Earth Day?*, http://video.foxnews.com/v/4657 163/student-indoctrination-to-honor-earth-day.

27. Doug Goodkin, *Earth Day Rap*, http://imet.csus.edu/imet2/stanfillj/workshops/music _in_curriculum/language_arts.htm/.

28. Fox News, *Student Indoctrination to Honor Earth Day?*, http://video.foxnews.com/v/4657 163/student-indoctrination-to-honor-earth-day.

29. Education Action Group, *MEAexposed.com: MESSA*, http://meaexposed.com/messa.

-###-

CPSIA information can be obtained at www.ICGtesting.com
Printed in the USA
LVOW071103121211

259020LV00002B/14/P